THE GROWTH QUOTIENT

How to achieve sustainable professional growth and development

SUBBARAO MUKKAVILLI

PROWESSCA
YOUR CAREER ACCELARATOR

EARLY RECOGNITION

The Growth Quotient: How to achieve sustainable professional growth and development by Suram is a useful manual that will guide readers to engineer their growth and let their critical skills take them to the top of the learning curve. The online exercises, activities, and psychometrics are good techniques to improve the analysis of situations and make appropriate choices. The author covers both the art and science of leadership and personal effectiveness, and the tips can be applied in the workplace. As we are aware, the corporate world is facing a shortage of good leaders and the strategies given in this book are a good way to enhance career prospects. The 4 critical elements required for sustained growth and success are useful and the exercises are good when it comes to picking up new skills and dropping the ones that are no longer needed. The book also helps to set long term meaningful goals and pursue them and also encourages readers to explore their inner self to identify good, bad, and undesirable habits.

The Growth Quotient: How to achieve sustainable professional growth and development by Suram is empowering and effective when it comes to teaching readers. Every chapter is packed with a lot of information, activities, and exercises to make them be on par with advancing technology, the power and possibilities of AI, machine learning and deep learning. Thanks to COVID-19, Robotic Process Automation has become very important. The approach to upgrading the brain is interesting and since the book is interspersed with exercises, psychometric tests, and activities, it is not boring. The tips and tools are simple to apply and practice and are also a good way to discover the self and see where changes need to be made. Reading this book helps to develop effective communication, and the author has dealt with the topics methodically, extensively, and expansively, giving clarity to the subject. It is a book for keeps as it can be used for reference and can be read and re-read to improve on The Growth Quotient.

Mamta Madhavan for Readers' Favorite

Written for a vast audience in the corporate sector including employees, entrepreneurs, team leaders, and business leaders, The Growth Quotient: How to achieve sustainable professional growth and development by Suram is an informative guide about growth, efficiency, preparedness, effectiveness and more. Chapter two of the work discusses how growth can be maintained and achieved in the context of ever-changing technological trends. Other topics discussed in the section include managing public personality/reputation and the aspects that contribute to a stable career. The fourth chapter discusses the external world and explains topics relating to communication, building relationships, client satisfaction, and others. Other chapters discuss broader topics divided into specific sub-topics and they include self-awareness, conflict resolution, digital trends, and data interpretation.

When reading Suram's The Growth Quotient, the infographics, psychometric tests, and charts were useful in helping me grasp the information contained in the book. Anecdotes and illustrations make the content interesting. This is further enhanced by the inclusion of engaging questions. In a world that is constantly changing, Suram provides practical tools that help in the process of growth. Various platforms that have revolutionized different industries, such as Canva, are discussed. The messages contained are encouraging such as why and how to get rid of unfounded fears or how to minimize weaknesses by working on and adding to strengths. Others are informative and unique such as the discussion on why it is important to filter information that gets to the mind as the mind does not have its own filter. The Growth Quotient provides useful business strategies for persons in the corporate world.

Edith Wairimu for Readers' Favorite

The Growth Quotient: How to achieve sustainable professional growth and development by Suram is a book for leaders who want to be effective in their jobs, especially in our business environment that is driven by rapidly growing technology. The author provides tools to help leaders become more effective in how they lead, and readers will discover the secret formula for doing more in less time, being more efficient, setting and meeting goals, developing new skills that help them take control of their financial and professional goals while deepening personal growth.

The book contains lessons and skills that readers need to stay focused and to accomplish what really matters and in an efficient way. The author brings a lot of experience and expertise into the writing, featuring online exercises and psychometrics designed to help readers scale their learning. One of the things I loved about this book is the author's ability to define why readers need to do what they need to do and the clear step-by-step guide when it comes to acquiring the skills. The "why" and the "how" of the message of this book is unmistakable. The writing is conversational and engaging. The author has the gift of communicating complex ideas in a clear and accessible manner. In a world filled with distractions, Suram teaches leaders how to thrive and successfully accomplish work that matters. While The Growth Quotient: How to achieve sustainable professional growth and development is written for leaders, it is a book with powerful messages for anyone who wants to drive positive results in both business and personal life. This is a book that anyone who wants to be an effective leader should read.

Jose Cornelio for Readers' Favorite

ISBN: **978-93-5407-935-1**

Created with Vellum

To my wife and children with love

CONTENTS

ACKNOWLEDGMENTS

"No duty is more urgent than that of returning thanks". — Anonymous

At the outset, I would like to thank my wife Annapurna, for standing by me throughout my career and helping me to become what I am today.

I would also like to thank my tiny twins Vishnu and Karthika for allowing me to steal the time I am supposed to give them.

I am grateful to my parents and brother for their constant support and encouragement throughout my journey.

A big thank you to my friend, Sridhar Kakarala for his constant help and feedback on the book.

I would not have been able to complete my book without their support and encouragement.

PREFACE

The planet we live in today spins and makes a full circle every twenty-four hours. No matter what we do, we move along, seamlessly.

However, what if one day, the world goes in one direction, and we do not move along with it? Disaster! Isn't it?

This is what is happening to most of us in the corporate world. We are oblivious to the motion and direction of the rest of the world. We are busy living inside an inbox. For some, it is Outlook, for others, it is WhatsApp or Facebook. We are thoroughly engrossed in them and yet we keep spinning and continue pushing ourselves to go with the flow.

So, how do we sense the motion and direction of the world, develop the necessary gravitational force and stay aligned to its movement? How do we track, and adapt to all the latest trends?

Fortunately, it is not very difficult. This book is all about helping you engineer your growth. My objective is to let your critical skills take you to the top of the learning curve.

Once you complete this course (book, online exercises, and psychometrics) successfully and practice all activities, people around you will notice a visible improvement in your ability to analyse a situation and make appropriate choices.

WHO IS THIS BOOK FOR?

Please ask yourself the following questions.

- Do you lead a team or wish to lead a team?
- Do you want to accelerate your career and be more in less time?
- Do want to learn the timeless secrets of leadership and stay updated?
- Do you want to be more productive and save two or more hours per day?
- Do you want to increase your efficiency and effectiveness?
- Do you have specific financial or professional goals?
- Are you wondering how to set a goal and track it?
- Do you wish to take charge of your life?
- Do you wish to improve your communication skills?
- Do you want to learn new-age skills and prepare yourself for the future?

If the answer is yes to three or more questions, then you will benefit from this book.

Additionally, ask yourself the following questions:

- I am willing to commit 30 minutes per day for 15 days for my growth.
- I agree that character values are the foundation of sustainable leadership.

I am going to teach you techniques that you can take to your desk and apply at your workplace. I have distilled the experience of my last thirty years and present them to you as tips, tricks, tools, traps, and hacks.

Mostly, I am going to cover both the art and science of leadership and personal effectiveness. Like any art, the concepts that you are going to learn here require concerted practice to perfect.

If you master all these techniques, you can save anything between 45 minutes to three hours each day. That's a whopping 1095 productive hours per year. Assuming you work ten hours a day, it is 109 man-days or close to four months a year.

What can you do with this extra time? You can pursue your passions, earn more money, clear outstanding debts faster or acquire your dream possessions.

ADDITIONAL INFORMATION

Register yourself on gem.prowessca.com to access various resources such as:

- Online course material
- How-to videos
- Worksheets
- Toolkits
- Presentation templates
- Latest developments and trends

Premium membership to the GEM Club will give you access to many more useful resources that will help you accelerate your career.

You can also find an e-learning version of this book on https://gem.prowessca.com

1

INTRODUCTION

"The illiterate of the 21st century will not be those who cannot read and write but those who cannot learn, unlearn and relearn..."

Alvin Toffler

AS THE OLD SAYING GOES, there are three types of people in this world: Those who make things happen, those who watch things happen, and those who wonder what happened.

During the last three decades of my career, I have been lucky to have worked with some of the best leaders in the corporate world across various sectors. While each of these leaders were unique, surprisingly, all of them shared certain distinct similarities.

. . .

At the same time, I have also interacted with several unsuccessful people. They were pseudo-professionals who always whined and contaminated the work environment. People under this category too shared some similarities.

Folks in the third category were blissful people who were oblivious to the movement of the planet. We will not discuss them much.

I have also observed a new category. People in the fourth category specialise in stopping things from happening. They are extremely creative in finding excuses and imagining problems. They possess an uncanny knack to convince their colleagues of their points. I observed an alarming increase in the number of such people particularly during the last decade. This could also be due to cultural diversity and generation gap.

No doubt, all of these types of people are beneficial for those around them, either because of their wisdom or due to their ignorance.

In this course (comprising the book, online exercises, and psychometric assessments,) I am going to explain the features of the people in each category. You will learn the secret strengths of the first category. I will explain why people in each category behave the way they do. You will also learn how to deal with people in other types.

Interestingly, most successful leaders are surrounded by followers belonging to other categories. Successful professionals face resistance and criticism from folks in the fourth category. But they manage to navigate their way through it and will reach their goals.

. . .

Authentic leadership emerges out of such adversities.

I will explain the qualities that separate a leader from a laggard. We will dissect each skill and trait that you need to learn, abandon or inculcate.

The corporate world is facing an acute shortage of good leaders. You will not only be able to make a difference but also enhance your career prospects significantly through this course.

You will understand the finer tenets of sophistication that will help engineer your growth.

We will explore four essential features of successful individuals. As you discover the vital skills, critical senses, core qualities and competencies of each of them, you will begin to understand yourself and the people around you.

During this journey, you will pick up several new skills and drop the ones you no longer need.

Chapter 2 gives you a broad overview of the current scenario and prepares you to cultivate a few essential qualities.

Chapter 3 helps you in exploring your inner self. You will understand various critical differentiating factors. You will also learn to identify several good, bad and undesirable qualities that you may harbour.

Chapter 4 is all about the external environment. You will pick up or polish important skills like communication, presentation, persuasion, conflict resolution, and motivation.

Chapter 5 takes you through the digital world and gives you a glimpse of what is likely to happen during the COVID pandemic and after. You will explore three critical dimensions of digital proficiency. You will get a bird's eye view of the current cyber threats and vulnerabilities.

Chapter 6 presents you with one of the vital senses that leaders will need in this VUCA (Volatility, Uncertainty, Complexity, and Ambiguity) world. In this chapter, you will learn what the data in your devices try to tell you and how you can amplify voices and listen to them clearly. Your ability to interpret data will give you a competitive edge and make you almost infallible.

Chapter 7 is a review of the topics covered, and lessons learned. You will also learn to set long-term meaningful goals and pursue them.

JOHARI WINDOW

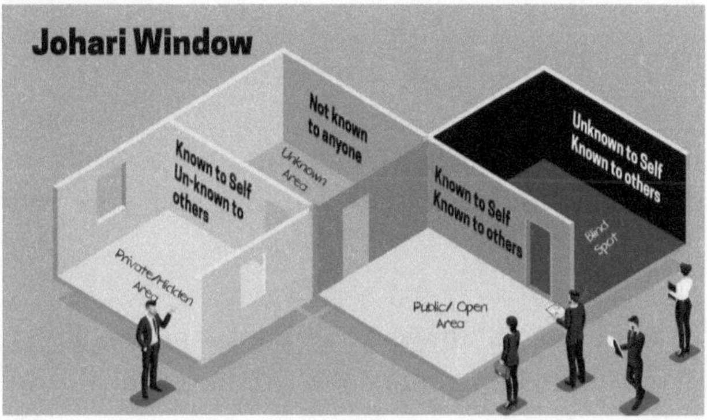

If you look at the Johari window carefully, you will realise that we are not aware of 75 percent of our true potential or weaknesses. We are completely ignorant of fifty percent of it. One-half lies hidden in a murky blind spot while the other waits to be discovered. Though we are conscious of the rest, it is never shared with the external world.

As part of us is never revealed to people around us, they are unable to recognise our potential and offer comments or suggestions on using it. That's a pretty bad state to be in; and it pretty much explains the interpersonal issues and conflicts we face every day.

. . .

I am going to concentrate on your unexplored areas and help you unlock your hidden potential. Trust me. You are sitting on a fortune. I will also describe the ways of taking feedback and thoroughly laundering the blind spots. If you follow the course sincerely, you will shine like an unblemished white canvas.

"Education consists mainly of what we have unlearned."
Mark Twain

We will also look at gradually opening up your personal area so that others can perceive and appreciate your hidden nature and talents.

After you work on all three, your public personality will shine through. We call it: Reputation. We will look into this in Chapter two.

There was once a confident robber who attempted a bank heist in broad daylight without a mask on in full view of the security cameras. He goes in to the bank and demands cash and gold and picks up everything he finds. He is proud of his success. As soon as he comes out, he gets caught by the police. Perplexed, he blurts out, " I applied lemon juice on my face!"

The robber firmly believed applying lemon juice on his face would do the same trick as it would to ink on a notebook. He would be invisible as long as he did not go near a heat source.

. . .

Why did the robber think that lemon juice could make him invisible? Why did he not test his assumption on some of his friends and family members?

Two social psychologists David Dunning and Justin Kruger were the first to research this.

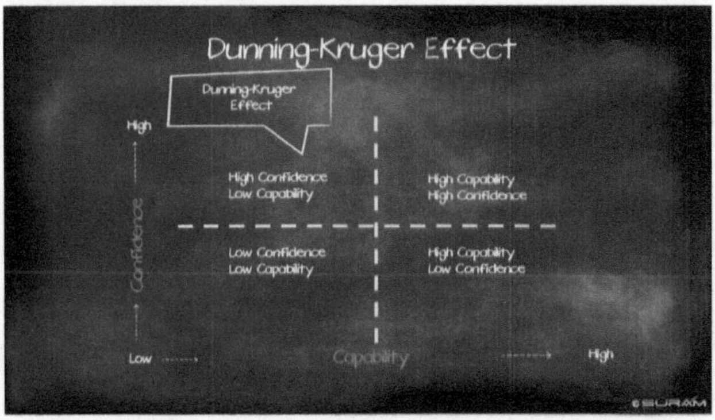

They called it the **'Dunning- Kruger Effect.'** As per the theory, a person with low capabilities is likely to feel that he is the smartest. He will be very confident of his skills. He assumes that he knows the subject better than anyone else on the planet. Does it ring a bell?

Intellectual humility

Scientists have been studying behavioural patterns like this to understand more about the triggers for such actions.

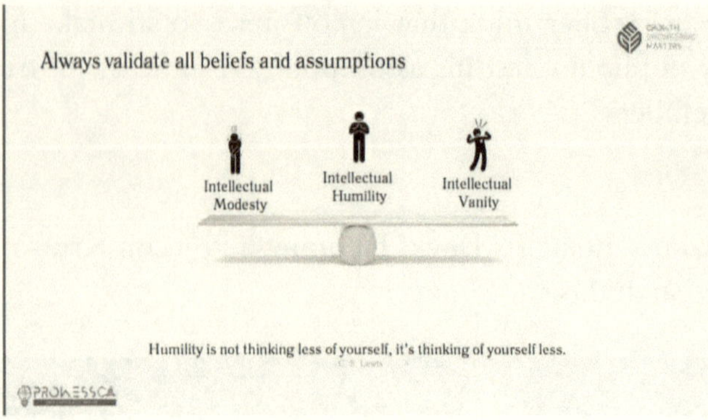

They found the following interesting facts:

- The intelligence we acquire over a period needs to be paired with humility. Humility makes us confident and curious, and prods us to validate our assumptions.
- If intelligence combines with modesty, we will be in self-doubt and consequently less confident.
- If the intelligence is coupled with vanity, we will be overconfident. There will be no scope for validation and all our assumptions will look like universal truths.

"Humility is not thinking less of yourself; it's thinking of yourself less."
C. S. Lewis

Scientists have also discovered that honey bees have high levels of cognitive capabilities and estimation skills.

Honeybees have the ability to collaborate with other bees in the group and make the right decisions. This is called 'swarm intelligence.' This kind of intelligence is being applied to robots using artificial intelligence algorithms. Swarm intelligence theory tells us that humans may have low estimation skills. This deficiency along with vanity and ego often generates the worst outcomes.

Ebbinghaus' forgetting curve

We all learn many things. We read books, watch videos, attend seminars and so on. Any content we consume will be first sent to a staging area in our brain and remain active for about twenty minutes. If you review the subject and mull over it within an hour, there are chances that you can recall and retrieve over 80 percent of what you learned.

If the subject is not reviewed, the retrieval capacity falls to 40 percent within 24 hours. Our brain will eventually remove the information completely, in a month.

There are a multitude of factors that impact brain function and retention. The increase in information load coupled with faulty eating and sleeping habits will cause the retention power to diminish quicker.

This is called **Ebbinghaus' forgetting curve.**

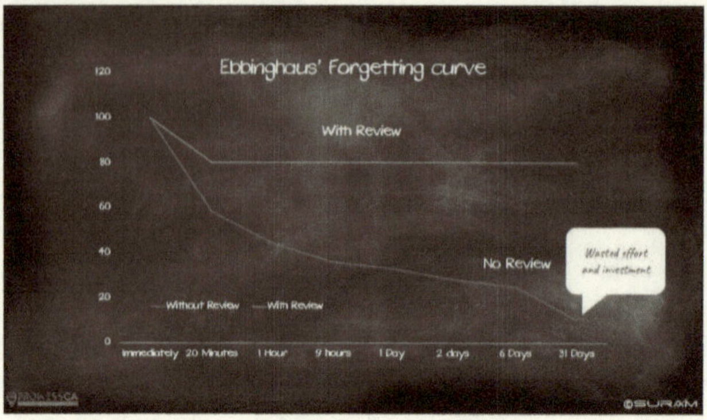

Obviously, this is a wasted time investment. What you think is important for you, should stay with you.

Therefore, you need to show commitment and review it periodically so that you don't lose the information.

I would urge you to learn, and review the concepts once within an hour.

Feynman technique

The best way to retain the information we acquire is by teaching it to someone. If you can explain a complex concept to a five-year-old, you have probably mastered it.

The famous scientist, Richard Feynman gave us a simple, four-step method:

- Pick a topic
- Explain it to a school child
- Identify gaps
- Review

I suggest you find a different child each time.

The easiest way to review is by recording your speech and listening to it again. Over a period of time:

- You would have built a large collection of audio books narrated by you
- You would have mastered the art of explanation; including public speaking
- You would have ensured 100 percent retention of all subjects you have learned

You know what to do after finishing this chapter.

My objective of explaining the concepts: Dunning Kruger Effect, Feynman technique and Forgetting curve, is to request you to adopt them for effective learning.

Learning objectives

At the end this book, you should be able to answer the following:

- Where are your roots for growth? How do you strengthen them?
- What is your 'reputation?' How do you want to shape it?
- How much time do you have? What is your act time balance?
- What are your innate strengths? What are the factors blocking those strengths?
- What shapes your personality?
- What kind of navigational tools do you need to always tread on the path of success?
- Who are the key people who matter to you? How do you support these stakeholders effectively and earn their support in return?
- How to identify and categorise team members to optimise productivity and engagement?

- What are the top ten virtues needed for success? How to acquire them?
- What sets the leaders and laggards apart?
- How to prioritise among multiple projects and handle all of them efficiently?
- How to foster open communication with team members?
- How to handle conflicts?
- How to improve your communication, presentation and public speaking skills?
- How to set wellness targets and pursue them meticulously?
- How to keep track of technology changes and stay competitive?
- How to be more productive?
- How to sense events as they happen or before they happen?
- How to achieve everyday effectiveness?

I wish you good luck.

2

GROWTH CONTEXT

"Don't go through life, grow through life."

Eric Butterworth

LEARNING objectives

At the end of this session, you will be able to:

- Appreciate the current market context
- Understand the need to manage your reputation
- Understand the roots of rapid and sustainable growth
- Appreciate the difference between skill and sense
- Identify the components of the core arsenal for a stable career
- Appreciate various technology trends that shape the future

- Understand the concept of 'Act Time Balance' and assess how much time you have
- Understand the four critical quotients required for a stable career
- Understand the total time available to you

We are living in an era of information and knowledge. The current environment is full of Volatility, Uncertainty, Complexity and Ambiguity. In short, it is a VUCA world. As if the abundant human ignorance (HI) is not sufficient, artificial intelligence (AI) is also on the rise. It is a double whammy. The competition is stern, and the values are lower than ever.

With rapid technology changes, business processes are changing fast, skills are getting obsolete sooner, and the increasing talent gap is competing with the population growth. In such a situation, how do you upgrade your talents and continue to stay competitive?

To be a successful leader, you need to possess 100+ skills and traits. To sustain the position, you have to give up 10 percent of these skills and acquire 20 percent additional expertise every year.

- How do you identify these required skills and behaviours?
- How do you learn and retain those?
- How do you blend and apply them to your workplace to ensure success every day?
- Are there any foundational competencies that will empower you to attract the rest of these success ingredients?

Fortunately, the answer is yes. Let's explore each of the possibilities now.

Mindsight

The world is changing rapidly. Most of the skillsets we use today will be irrelevant very soon. Several jobs that exist today will be extinct. AI-powered apps and robots will replace all of them.

The corona pandemic has fast-tracked most of these developments. COVID-19 is rewriting the rules of the game, and AI is automating them. Acute talent deficiency is another pandemic all of us will face very soon.

Ok. Let us park the topic of pandemics for some time and talk about our eyesight. Here is a quick overview of our sight.

The average human eyesight is around 20 by 20. People with 20/30 vision don't get a driving license in most countries. Anything around 20/1000 is considered blindness. No light perception is called total blindness. On the contrary, hawks have a 20/2 vision.

Now, what about our mindsight? Is it 20/20? More? If so, is it sufficient? The answer is no to all questions.

The 'mindsight' of an average corporate worker will be around 20/800. Yes, 20/800. That means near blindness or no light perception. In this case, it is called 'no data perception.' They cannot comprehend what they see. The ability to make sense of data and information is almost negligible. They cannot sense even an avalanche until it fully hits them. This condition is called 'mind blindness'.

Some of the world's massive fires could have been controlled with just two mugs of water, had they been detected at the right time.

If you are not convinced, let us estimate the mindsight of the key functionaries in our governments. What does the corona situation tell us? Do you agree that they had a chance to detect this early and prevent the spread of COVID-19?

This book is all about improving your mindsight.

It introduces four different lenses to you. They can improve your mindsight significantly.

You need to use different lenses for different situations. We will discuss this in the next section.

Technology trends

Changing job landscapes and growing skill gaps

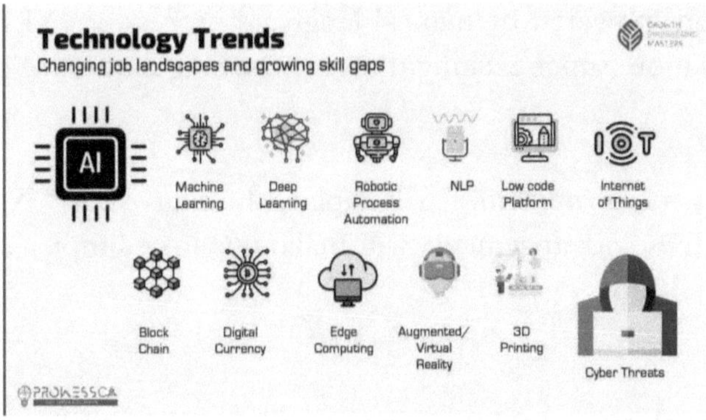

Technology is changing rapidly.

Whether the corona virus has changed our lifestyles or not, it has changed the pace of technology. It is a new era of technology now. The BC era or 'before the corona' era, though extensive, was not very exciting. Now, the WC (with corona) era and AC (after corona) era will trigger rapid developments in technology.

I have been part of IT /ITES industry for over 30 years now. I have seen many things change. Now, I am confident of seeing three-fold growth in the next three years. What I witnessed in the last 30 years was only a trailer for the main blockbuster.

The world is slowly realising the power and possibilities of AI. Machine learning and deep learning are becoming pervasive. Deep learning enables us to replicate human capabilities in machines so that humans could be upgraded to better jobs.

Thanks to COVID, Robotic Process Automation has taken a prime seat. We will have many more voice and natural language-based transactions powered by natural language processing (NLP). There are many more super exciting things happening in the world.

Does this mean machines will replace humans soon? Not at all. Each of these advancements will make our lives simpler and open up more jobs.

Trust me; during the 90s, when emails and mobiles were introduced, several people went into panic mode. They complained about privatisation and what not. Look at what has happened now. We are becoming better by the day with technology.

Of course, each of these advancements will result in substantial skill gaps. As I speak now, there are several new open positions in the technology space. Technology is not just information technology.

This planet has a vast pool of educated workers, but over 98 percent of them need to be either re-skilled or up-skilled. So the skill gap is enormous. It is only going to widen.

But understand one thing for the rest of your life. **The gap presents an opportunity. A wider gap means an enormous opportunity.** I repeat. An enormous opportunity.

The only problem we face now is our inability to upgrade our brains in tandem with these advancements. This shortcoming is creating frustration, panic, and unwanted anxiety.

. . .

We will take a deep dive into each of these developments when we talk about technology in the later chapters.

I will also provide several tips, tools and techniques to upgrade the brain and get re-skilled to grab hold of these opportunities.

The situation seems super scary. But believe me, we can convert it to a super exciting journey. Many people have done it and some are still doing it. You can also do it. I will ensure you do it. Let's proceed.

What is not changing?

So many things change. Is there anything that does not change and remains constant for ages? Yes. Our brains. The way we think. The way we react, and our expectations. None of them change.

The human expectation of getting more for less never changes.

We want all our calls to be answered in less than a second. We want the customer support executive to treat us like the American president. We want food served in an instant. We want instant responses from others. Instant phone recharges.

We want high-quality products and services at low prices delivered at lightning speed. We expect strong emotional support. All these traits are always constant and permanent.

My grandfather had the same obsession. I continue to harbour the same desires and my grandson too may do the same and the cycle will continue. This is one area where no training intervention is needed.

Mr. Jeff Bezos once said:

"I very frequently get the question: 'What's going to change in the next ten years?'

And that is a very interesting question; it's a very common one.

I almost never get the question: 'What's not going to change in the next ten years?'

And I submit to you that that second question is the more important of the two because you can build a business strategy around the things that are stable in time. In our retail business, we know that customers want low prices, and I know that's going to be valid ten years from now. They want fast delivery; they want vast selection. It's impossible to imagine a future ten years from now where a customer comes up and says, 'Jeff I love Amazon; I just wish the prices were a little higher,' [or] 'I love Amazon; I just wish you'd deliver a little more slowly.' Impossible. And so the effort we put into those things, spinning those things up, we know the energy we put into it today will still be paying off dividends for our customers ten years from now. When you have something that you know is true, even over the long term, you can afford to put much energy into it."

YOUR 'ACT TIME' BALANCE

Imagine that you are stranded in a deep forest. It is getting dark and you have no means of finding a way out.

. . .

You are only left with a mobile that has less than five percent battery charge. You are desperate to call your family and alert them to help you. You are searching for a suitable place to get good signal strength. Suddenly, you get a call from someone you don't have a good relationship with. That person argues with you about something that is not very important. You get frustrated and prolong the argument. After ten minutes, you realise that the mobile is running out of battery and the call will disconnect.

It strikes you that you have less than one percent charge left, and it's too late to make a call.

Do you get into the same situation in this concrete jungle as well? How often? Most of us think that we have plenty of time. But how much time do you believe we have to pursue a goal?

Bang comes the response, "Oh! We are all immortals."

Let's say, you want to pursue a new skill or hobby. Or you want to plan for your life's ambitions. Let's calculate the time once:

Sundays. : 52
Saturdays : 52
Public holidays : 15
Paid leaves : 21
Meetings : 104
Non-productive days : 20
Total 'gone with the wind' days. : 264
Left-out days : 101
Average number of productive hours per day : 4

Balance working years: **20**
Total hours left to act: **8,080***

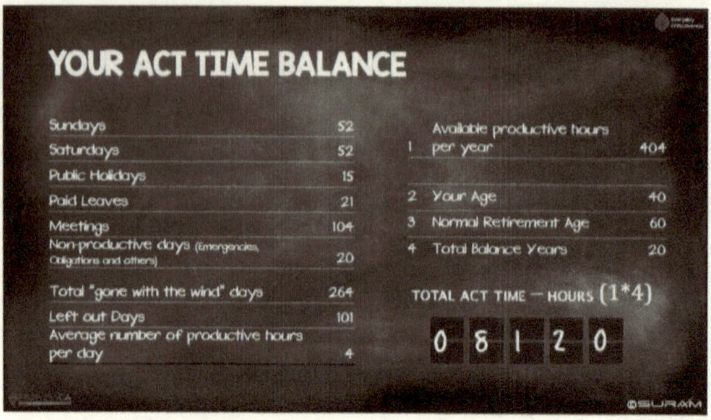

* Assuming that you are able to maintain the grit to stay focused for four hours a day to pursue your ambition.

Is it a good balance? What can we accomplish in 400 hours? What is your current reputation? What do you want it to be?

REPUTATION

Long ago, there was a young boy who hailed from a low-income family. His father was an accomplished engineer and an expert in making machine tools and explosives.

Inspired by his father, this young boy developed a passion for chemistry and engineering. He also enjoyed the process of manufacturing explosives, and in due course, this young boy grew up to be a successful scientist. He also had a friend who invented nitroglycerine, a substance used as an explosive.

Nitroglycerine is an unpredictable and unsafe material for commercial use. Though his friend warned the young man about the potential dangers of his invention, he went on to research the sensitive material further. He subsequently emerged as a successful entrepreneur and an accomplished scientist with over 350 patents. Everything was going well for this commercially successful scientist.

. . .

Unfortunately, one day, there was an explosion in the quarry. His brother passes away in the quarry mishap. The local newspaper erroneously carries the obituary of the entrepreneur. He wakes up the next day to find headlines about his death. They say, "The merchant of death is dead. The man who became rich by finding ways to kill more people faster than ever before, died yesterday." He is shaken by what he reads and starts repenting. He donates over 95 percent of his wealth to constitute prizes for eminence in five faculties irrespective of the nationality of the recipients. The prize money today roughly equals 500 million USD.

Today, we call them Nobel Prizes, and the man referred to was none other than Dr. Alfred Nobel.

What does the story of Alfred Nobel tell us? Well, many things! The most important takeaway is that we need to continually protect our reputation while growing to reach newer heights.

The fame of successful people outlasts their lives. Though the physical body gets destroyed at some point, their popularity continues to shine for decades or even centuries.

When you think of a scientist, who do you recall from the top of the mind? Chances are that you thought of Einstein.

When you think of an astronaut, whose name comes to mind first? Chances are that you were reminded of Neil Armstrong.

Similarly, when you think of other specialists like doctors, lawyers or teachers who do you remember first and why?

. . .

Step back and ask yourself. What are you famous for? What do you want to be famous for? From when? Till when?

At this stage, what do people remember you for? Does that align with your desires? Is it in sync with your life's purpose?

How are people benefiting from you? By your wisdom or by your ignorance?

We must make wise choices about our lives and align our goals accordingly. It is ideally done during the early part of the career. The good news is that I am here to assist you entirely in this process. During this journey, I will help you to make these choices wisely.

Having a meaningful goal is the first step.

What do you want to acquire? What are those prized possessions? Is it a fancy car? Luxurious home? A good bank balance? All of them? None of them?

Remember, your real assets are always intangible. Knowledge, health and relationships are your real wealth and possessions for you to take pride in. The rest of the belongings are transitory and worthless. The above three possessions will set you free while other material possessions lock you up.

FOUNDATIONAL TRAITS

"A man's worth is no greater than his ambitions."
Marcus Aurelius

Three aspects define your personality:

- What you have
- What you drop
- What you pick

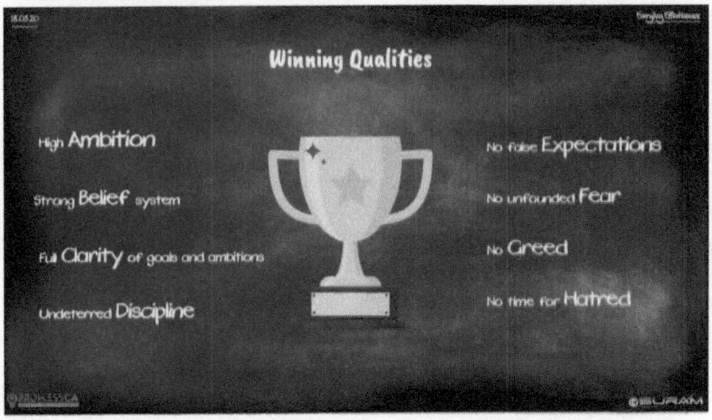

The foundational qualities you need to have:

- High **ambition**
- A strong **belief** system
- **Clarity** on goals and ambitions
- Undeterred **discipline**

ABCDs in short.

The thoughts you need to drop:

- Unrealistic **expectations**
- Unfounded **fear**
- **Greed**
- H**atred**

Ambition

It all starts with ambition. It is the fuel that can transform potential energy into kinetic energy. We all have desires and drives. I wrote this book because of my ambition to teach someone. You are reading it because of your ambition to learn something new. We always want to do something better.

Ambition is believing in yourself, even when no one else in the world does. We need to have the ambition to create the drive, grit and determination to succeed.

Belief

"If you don't stand for something, you will fall for anything."
Anonymous

We are not talking about faith or anything close to religion. We are talking about the conditioning of our brain to embrace success and realise one's purpose.

"Believe you can, and you're halfway there."
Theodore Roosevelt.

An ordinary person sees something and believes it. An extraordinary person believes in something and shows it to the world. Walt Disney had visualised Disneyland long before it was built. Steve Jobs had played with iPhones mentally much before they were physically produced. If you want to make a difference, you need to believe in your ideas first.

Before you can become successful, you need to believe that you can become successful. You need to build the right beliefs and fence them with your core values. Practicing core values will protect your beliefs.

- You are what you believe
- Your belief creates your vision
- Vision builds meaningful goals
- Goals trigger passion

A healthy belief system enables you to make your dreams come true. If you don't build on your dreams, someone will use you to build on their dreams.

. . .

Clarity

> "It's a lack of clarity that creates chaos and frustration. Those emotions are poison to any living goal."
>
> Steve Maraboli

No, we are not talking about the clarity on larger life issues like finding your purpose or becoming a mystic. We are also not talking about finding out how the president is going to handle the global crisis.

We are just talking about the clarity of :

- Your role
- The jobs you handle
- Delivering what you are accountable for
- Predictability of crucial people you work with or work for
- Visibility of fundamental changes or trends that are likely to impact you and your team

The first step in finding answers to these questions is by simply changing a preference that is, by developing a craving for clarity.

When you develop a desire for clarity, the magic begins to happen. The need to have clarity will not let you make assumptions, procrastinate or leave anything untidy or disorganised. When you have clarity, the next logical step is following it up with action.

- Be clear about yourself.
- Find clarity about the preferences and priorities of your clients, boss, direct reports, and other key stakeholders.
- Declutter your home, office room, laptop, mind, and heart. Purity sparks clarity.
- Ensure that there are no open assumptions about anything you are accountable to manage.
- Understand the hums of data.
- Avoid procrastination.
- Ascertain the predictability of crucial people.
- Watch out for visible fundamental changes and trends.

Discipline

- Discipline is what binds everything together.
- It teaches you how to be accountable.
- Discipline is a magic ingredient of life that can transform the ordinary into extraordinary.

Discipline to our mind is what the Sun is to this planet. It's free, consistent and extremely crucial. Imagine a week without sunlight. There is no bigger calamity to the world? Multiple fuels can power our execution engines: discipline, motivation, curiosity, emotion and passion.

You will quickly notice that fuels like motivation are not only temporary but are also costly. If your engine is running on motivation, it is on a high maintenance mode. The engine encounters frequent breakdowns and requires expensive fixes. The same is the case with all other fuels. They are even costlier and available in fewer quantities. Discipline is the best fuel that will ignite and run the execution engine in you. You can occasionally mix them up and give a nitro boost to your engine. However, if you take discipline out, you will encounter a sudden breakdown on your race track. You won't win the race for sure; and you could also be overtaken by your competitor who may be on the 'D' fuel.

- Add it to your talent list, you'll become competent.
- Add it to an idea: It will transform into a well-executed project.
- Put it in a child: You get a prodigy.
- Put it in an ordinary man: You'll get a professional.
- Add it to a goal: You get accomplishment.
- Similarly, take discipline out of any professional and the person becomes dull and lazy. He will languish every day and eventually perish.

> "Seek freedom and become captive of your desires. Seek discipline and find your liberty."
>
> – Frank Herbert

All human beings come pre-fitted with a powerful 'execution engine' that enables them to act on something. It is the same engine that drives us to drink that first drop of milk, stand on our feet or take that first step. Our bodily movements are results of physical manoeuvres, not ideas.

. . .

All successful people in the world upgrade this engine into a high-power monster. All unsuccessful people neglect it or spoil it completely. There is no other differentiation. But why do these engines break down? Discipline is about doing what must be done, even if you don't want to do it.

Expectation

"Expectations were like fine pottery. The harder you held them, the more likely they were to crack."

Brandon Sanderson

It hits you hard when you think you are important to someone, and they prove you wrong.

When you stop expecting people to be perfect, you will like them for who they are. If you expect nothing from anybody, you will never be disappointed. In the next section, we will look at the reasons for having expectations and also how to set others' expectations about you.

"Life shrinks or expands in proportion to one's courage."
Anais Nin

Fear

Fear kills more dreams than failure. Fear does not stop death. It stops life.

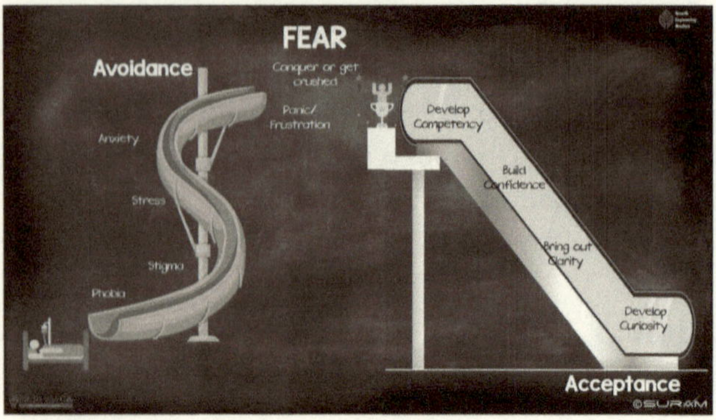

We are not talking about being fearless while doing something illegal and unethical.

We are talking about the fears you may have developed that are controlling a large part of your life. An unfounded fear might look like a risk aversion mechanism but it has severe implications on your health, prospects, and even your position in the society.

For some people, fear might work as a stimulant. If you are not afraid of your boss, you may not stick to the timelines. But that's not something that needs to be controlled or stimulated by fear. You need to develop a discipline and strengthen your values to avoid making such mistakes.

The point is to be a bit sceptical to avoid being cheated by situations.

If you are avoiding activities that you are expected to do to prosper; it is a problem. It will breed anxiety, stress, frustration, and tons of negativity. Sometimes fear can manifest itself as hatred or phobia. These cases might require psychiatric interventions.

In the next session, we will do a deep dive into various types of fears and we will learn how to conquer them.

Are you SAD? You may have Stress, Anxiety and Depression?

Do you have Fear, Uncertainty and Doubt (FUD) Fatigue?
You may be harbouring Fear, Uncertainty and Doubt.

Greed

> "There is no fire like passion, and there is no shark like hatred; there is no snare like folly; there is no torrent like greed."
>
> Siddhartha Gautama

Greed is the breeding ground for several unethical and immoral acts. A greedy person feels a false sense of entitlement. He'll seek fulfilment at the cost of another person's primary need.

In the next section, we will discuss the internal enemies of our well-being. Greed takes the primary position far ahead of the others.

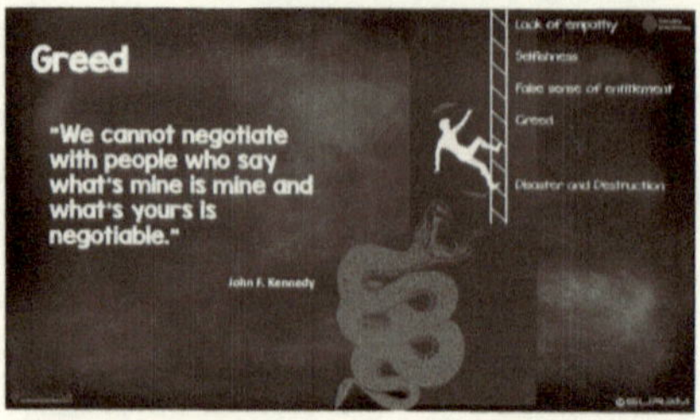

Many times, most of the bad qualities are considered good when they are in moderation and for a cause. For example, a reasonable amount of fear may be beneficial. Similarly, anger, desire, envy are necessary in moderate quantities.

Greedy people don't know when to come out of an investment, gamble, or just about anything they start.

Hatred

Hatred is a form of self-punishment. It stems from a lack of clarity and is a severe problem born out of a lack of a more significant purpose. To sum it up, it is very critical to get rid of these four negative energies from your mind to free it up to attract something positive and useful.

THE GROWTH QUOTIENTS.

Many managers in the corporate world think that their employees need to have Intelligence Quotient and Emotional Quotient to be successful. These two quotients were no doubt helpful until the last decade. But it is no longer the case in this era of the **fourth industrial revolution.**

Large and successful organisations realise that all their leaders need to possess a third quotient as well. This is called Digital Quotient.

. . .

However, very few people know that there is a hidden fourth quotient that plays a significant role in our personality development, growth prospects, and the proper development of the rest of quotients.

Yes. Such a powerful quotient has been hiding for a very long time. It is the Consciousness Quotient. None of the other three quotients can be leveraged effectively without acquiring the consciousness quotient.

1. Consciousness quotient
2. Environmental quotient
3. Digital Quotient
4. Number Quotient

Consciousness Quotient gives you nano-lenses through which, you can perceive self-awareness. Self-awareness is critical to acquire the rest of the quotients.

Environmental Quotient provides us a lens that helps us assess the ecosystem around us. This could include our team, clients, other people, policies, or trends – in short, the whole environment. Traditional EQ is a subset of this.

Digital Quotient gives you another set of advanced lenses that enables us to fine-tune three dimensions of tech-savviness: self, workplace, and family.

. . .

Number Quotient enables us to make sense of the data we see. The more you acquire this, the lesser you will be at the risk of mind-blindness. Intelligence Quotient is a subset of this quotient.

All these quotients are collectively called **Growth Quotients.**

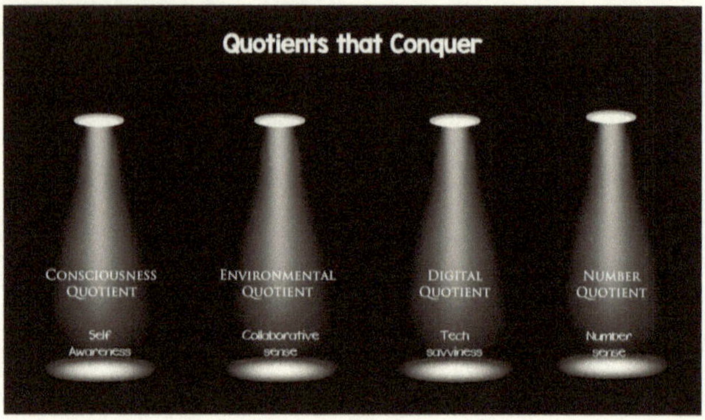

In the next four chapters, we will discuss self-connect, external connect, tech connect and number connect. Each of them corresponds to the four quotients. In short, we need to pick the STEN skills.

I have come to you with several practical tips and simple methods so that you can grasp the key concepts and put them to use at your workplace. Once you master these principles and apply them to your workplace, you should be able to reap rich productivity and efficiency benefits.

To sum up, these three aspects define your personality:

- What you have - ABCD
- What you drop - EFGH
- What you pick - STEN

SUMMARY

- Manage these four vitamins, and you can manage the rest of the world.
- A positive attitude is your gateway to joy.
- Tune your belief system. The world will dance to your tunes.
- Clarity is about connecting with your inner self first and then refining your dialogue with others.
- Discipline is the primary driver of your fate.
- Reflect on your reputation.
- Use your act time balance wisely.
- Drop expectations, fear, greed and hatred.
- Intelligence and emotional quotients are no longer sufficient to be successful in this competitive world.
- We need to possess digital quotient.
- Consciousness is the key to all above.

Questions

- Which is the most important of all four quotients?
- Which is the most harmful quality that we need to lose?
- Which of these traits will take us farther?

3

SELF-AWARENESS

"Wisdom tends to grow in proportion to one's awareness of one's ignorance."

– Anthony de Mello

IN THIS SESSION, we are going to explore self-awareness.

LEARNING OBJECTIVES

At the end of this session, you will be able to:

- Understand the need to acquire self-awareness
- Appreciate the urgency to install a Mind Positioning System
- Explore various critical components of Mind Positioning System

- Understand why different people react differently to a same adversity
- Realise that the brain is controlled by 'resistance twins'
- Learn how to overcome fear and greed
- Understand different types of motivations
- Learn how to set and pursue goals
- Differentiate between a skill and a sense
- Learn how to develop mental toughness
- Understand the ten virtues and eleven evils
- Learn how to move out of comfort zones

THE INNER-NET

- We surf the internet for several hours a day. When do we surf our inner-net?
- We frequently and passionately upgrade all our possessions be it clothes, shoes or gadgets. For convenience's sake, we will not talk about mobiles.
- All this is fine, but when did we last upgrade our brain?
- We meet several people during the day, whether we need to or not.
- When did we last meet that most important person? You know that the person in the mirror is the most important person. The more familiar you are with them, the more they will support you. The more support this person offers, the more robust and sturdier you will turn out to be. You need a lot of help from this person.
- We gift several things to various people. We also receive many gifts in return.
- Ask yourself: when did you gift yourself something lasting and exciting? No, we are not talking about mobile and gadgets.
- How are you spending your act time balance?
- What do you do before breakfast?

Can you name a few self-made men or women?

- Steve Jobs?
- Abraham Lincoln?
- Nightingale?

None. We must appreciate that there is no concept of a self-made man or woman. Behind every successful person, there is a large team for sure. How do they create such vibrant teams? Is it through position and power? No. All of them are natural leaders.

If you understand yourself well, you can manage yourself well. Better management of yourself unravels a more energetic personality. People with firm and strong personalities can manage the external world better.

What are your strengths? How do you maximise and leverage those?

What are your shortcomings, weaknesses, and fears? How do you overcome those?

PERSONALITY PROFILING

Do we need to always worry about our fears and weaknesses only? The answer is a straight no.

. . .

We should minimise them. We should conquer our fears and bridge skill gaps but we should always highlight our positives and play to our strengths.

Look at any straight line. How do we make a straight line shorter and thinner without touching it?

We learn this in primary school. By drawing another longer line next to it. Strengths and weaknesses work on a similar principle. The best way to minimise your weaknesses is by maximising your strengths.

But first you need to understand what your strengths and weaknesses are. Accept that we have flaws and apply the 4T principle (Terminate-Transfer-Treat-Tolerate) to reduce the risks.

Next, we need to identify the strengths and work on them further to maximise them.

If everyone can play against the strengths of others, there will be very healthy competition instead of dangerous conflicts. Everyone will be highly motivated and deliver results with high self-esteem.

There will be no blame games, politics or regrets. Knowing more about yourself will help you achieve more. Ok, but how do we identify our strengths?

I would like to introduce four essential and useful psychometric tools for you. These tools help you discover yourself and the people around you. They will help you develop the critical pillars necessary for your growth:

- Dominant personality traits
- Character and values
- Professional strengths
- Key personality types

Let's look at each one of them.

OCEAN

The OCEAN test or the Big Five personality test measures five crucial aspects of our personality

- Openness
- Conscientiousness
- Extraversion
- Agreeableness
- Neuroticism

Openness

Openness is all about how curious and open-minded you are to engage with anything new.

Whether it is a new project, initiative or experience.

. . .

A person who is high in openness is generally curious. He accepts non-conventional ideas and has high levels of creativity.

People with low openness are conventional, consistent, and cautious. Therefore, they have low creativity levels.

Conscientiousness

Conscientiousness is all about how organised and dependable you are. How does one become dependable?

They need to

- Be very organised.
- Pay good attention to detail.
- Be efficient and effective.

So those who score high on this parameter will have all the above qualities. They will have a desire to complete their tasks on time. Therefore, they will ask the right questions, clarify assumptions, and will also set the expectations upfront. There is no scope of ambiguity with such people. Their discipline levels will be very high.

These people come well-prepared for the meetings. They will not commit to anything without a concrete plan.

. . .

People who rate low in conscientiousness are laid back. They are disorganised, undependable and negligent.

Extraversion

Extroverted people are friendly, fun-loving and talkative. They enjoy social interactions and tend to be assertive if need be.

They are the ones who start a conversation. High scorers tend to be sociable, friendly, fun-loving and talkative while those who score low are introverted, reserved, inhibited and quiet. People who are low in extraversion are more reserved and prefer to stay calm.

Agreeableness

Agreeableness is all about team spirit and adjustment. People who are high on agreeableness are the least fussy and accommodative. They are the people who are involved in the least amount of conflicts because they value the relationships more than their viewpoints.

They are kind, compassionate, and considerate. They also forgive and forget quickly. This means that they have the best attitude and strong resilience. These people trust others and are trustworthy.

Low scorers whine, crib and thrive on criticism and callousness. This could be because they are more analytical and detached.

. . .

Neuroticism

Unlike the other traits, a high score in neuroticism implies that you drive people crazy. People who are highly neurotic are prone to stress, anxiety and insecurity. They are hypersensitive to feedback and even a tinge of criticism.

Low scores in other traits indicate that you are struggling with something. A high score on neuroticism means that people around you are suffering because of you.

People with low neuroticism are calm and composed. We don't know if they feel secure but they undoubtedly can make people around them feel so. Please take this test. It is quite interesting and revealing. Login to gem.prowessca.com and follow the prompts.

OTHER PSYCHOMETRIC TESTS

VIA Character Strengths

The next psychometric test is about the character.

Character is about doing the right thing when nobody is watching. It is the real foundation of your success. A man could have wealth, health, power, and many more treasures in abundance. But if he lacks character, he is equal to a dead man.

VIA Institute on Character has listed 24 core character strengths. These core characters determine your success, respect, progress and many such aspects.

. . .

They offer one basic psychometric test and four detailed profile reports. The basic version is free and can tell you about the hidden strengths you hold. I strongly recommend that you pause for a while, take this test and return with your results.

https://www.viacharacter.org/survey/account/register

GALLUP/CLIFTON STRENGTH FINDER

While the VIA test is about the character strengths, the Clifton test is about your talents. There are 34 signature themes that Clifton Strengths finder can uncover and the test identifies five dominant themes.

Unfortunately, Clifton site does not have a free version of the test. But it may be okay to spend a few dollars on finding your true talents. I have been doing this for the last 12 years. I take this assessment every two or three years. There are visible changes in the strengths and talents I imbibe from time to time.

You can access this on https://www.gallup.com.

As I mentioned earlier, I am not affiliated with any of these, nor do I get any returns from anyone.

16 Personalities

. . .

As per this metric, all the people on the planet fall under one of the 16 different personality types. The classification is based on how we interact, perceive information, judge a situation and so on.

While we need to pay for the Myers-Briggs Type Indicator (MBTI) test, we have a basic version available for free at www.16personalities.com.

MIND

Whenever we are hungry, our stomach sends multiple signals to the whole body.

Immediately, our eyes start the search operation, and our tongue joins the mission triggering the taste filters, the nose further supports with the smell filter, mouth secretes saliva, and so on.

The entire body works in tandem until we finish a plate or two. Most of the time, over-cooperation results in binging.

If for some reason, the food is not tasty or is toxic, the stomach rejects and returns it immediately.

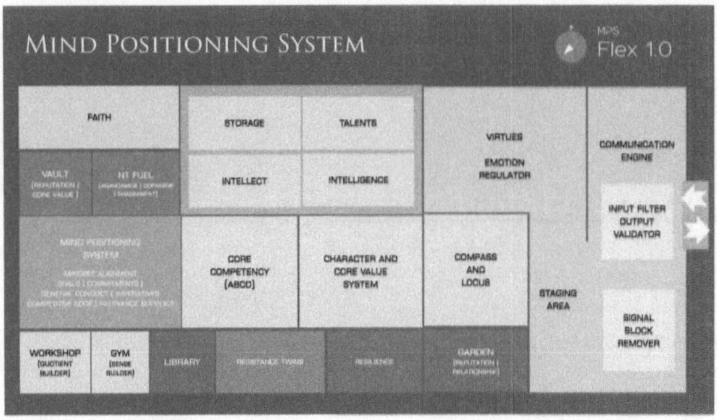

But have you noticed? Our brain does not experience hunger pangs. Our sensory organs send out no signals when the brain needs fodder. The eyes are quiet, and the ears do not bother to cooperate. There is no filtering and rejection mechanism. The brain quietly takes in all the toxic information without fuss.

However, as it cannot experience similar pangs, the brain also starves and develops indigestion over time. The outcome is that the brain cannot differentiate, assimilate or hold the attention span for more than a few seconds. There are theories that a starfish has a better attention span than humans.

Is it a manufacturing defect? Well, we will question the manufacturer when we meet him. But until then, we need to work on it.

There is a need to install some of these sensors, filters, and support aids. There is a need to flex some of those muscles until the functions return to acceptable levels.

. . .

Since we are refurbishing, let us also add a couple of more sensors and navigational tools.

Let's call it the Mind Positioning System.

Fortunately, this is available in the world and has been tried and tested on numerous people.

You will be surprised to know that there are three versions. Yes, like an iPhone, it comes in basic, max, and pro max models.

Max and pro max are out of our reach, at least for some time. We will look at the basic flex version.

After we start using the basic version, we will suddenly feel as if we have acquired superpowers. Our effectiveness and efficiency levels go up. Our relationships improve and our attention span goes through the roof. Many more positive things will happen to you. Where can we find examples of this? All successful individuals have this.

Let us find out more details about it.

By the way, are you curious about the max and pro max versions? I have met people who have used the max version. They can read people like a book. They have the highest levels of intuition and something that can only be described as a powerful sixth sense.

. . .

What about pro max? Well, people who have tried this version possess supernatural abilities like telepathy, and clairvoyance. They could just place their hands on the book and can comprehend the whole book. Whenever a person walks into the room, they will instantly read the traits and intentions of that person. This is not available on the fiction books also.

I have read about the people with these capabilities. Their abilities seem supernatural, mystical even.

THE MIND POSITIONING SYSTEM FLEX 1.0

Let's explore the components of our Mind Positioning System (MPS).

At the forefront, we have communication channels and a communication engine. Think of it as a security check process. We have two main functions here:

- Input /output filter and validator
- Signal block remover

Both these modules ensure that we only enter a clean input and get a complete output free of wrong signals, assumptions and inhibitions. Once these two checks are completed, the message moves to the staging area.

Here, you have the top ten virtues and an emotion regulator. This module ensures that we don't respond to anything before we comprehend, prepare, and pack.

. . .

We have several other components that are responsible for specific functions. We will explore each element in detail in this chapter. Once we finish discovering all the components, we will revisit this diagram.

TEN VIRTUES

As per the ancient Indian Vedic system, there are ten signature virtues. These ten strengths determine your personality and your professional and spiritual success.

They are:

- Fortitude
- Perseverance
- Focus
- Learning
- Purity
- Restraint
- Confidence
- Truthfulness
- Intellect
- Forgiveness

- The first virtue is **fortitude**. Fortitude is about staying confident during tough times. It is about believing in our strengths and staying courageous.
- **Perseverance** is the seminal strength one must possess to stay put on any chapter one has opened. Without determination, there is no endurance. You will give up at the first sight of a problem.

- A strong **focus** is the key to developing the required strengths. Only with an unwavering focus, can you unify and converge all energies. If every moving object is a target for you, you will be called promiscuous.
- **Continuous learning** is essential for sustained success. The day you stop learning, is the day you stop living. The physical body might exist, but it will be without any life or energy.
- The **purity** of thought, mind, and body are the fundamental hygiene essentials of life. While the epidemic has taught us to purify the body, we are yet to master how to purify our mind.
- Showing **restraint** and aiming for long-term gratification is the key to accomplish anything enduring and worthwhile. Several great people on this planet are remembered every day. Their reputation outlives their life. All such personalities have one thing in common. They are not lured by the short-term or immediate gratifications. They also put physical comforts at the end of their priority list.
- Having **confidence**, is having a life. It's not about whether you fall; it's all about whether you can pick yourself up afterwards.
- Be **truthful**, and you will be known as a trustworthy leader. Give room for the slightest of doubts, you will be equated to a selfish politician. That will spell doom for your career. Period.
- **Intellect** is about having the ability to be just and maintain discretion. It is about the ability to identify and differentiate the good from the bad. If everyone appears the same and all roads look the same, the path you take will only lead you to an endless pit.
- **Forgiveness** is the most critical virtue you need to practice. It saves time, earns friends, melts foes, improves your health, enhances your trustworthiness, and earns you more laurels than anything else I can imagine.

You must cultivate these habits and practice them every hour until they become your nature.

The virtue of character is a mean between two vices. One of excess and one of deficiency.

GREAT PERSONALITIES

Look at these great personalities. Do you think they practiced these virtues? If so, how many of them?

THE ELEVEN EVILS

Ever wondered what powers the stupidity in us? While some folks are super stupid, others are tolerably so. So what breeds this stupidity?

Our mind is afflicted continuously by eleven evils:

- Envy
- Anger

- Greed
- Desire
- Obsession
- Arrogance
- Aversion
- Ego
- Attraction
- Inhibition
- Ignorance

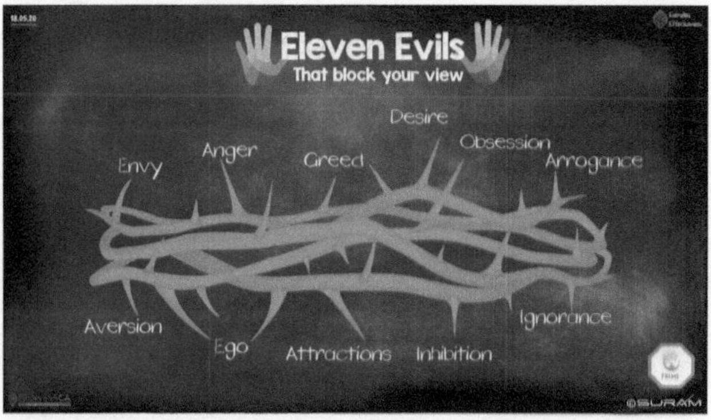

These eleven players keep playing a cricket match in our brain all the time. But the games these eleven evils play are distracting and destructive.

Whenever someone is speaking, one or all these 11 players spring up and weaken our signals. What we receive is only a distorted message that is often toxic.

They always hum in our brains and contaminate our thought processes. The result? You take in and spew out rubbish.

. . .

What happens when arrogance runs its course? We don't want to listen or comprehend. Remember the lemon juice story and the Dunning-Kruger Effect?

Greed is a breeding ground for several unethical and immoral acts. A person with greed feels a false sense of entitlement. He seeks fulfilment at the cost of another person's basic needs.

Greed takes precedence over everything else.

There may be a few times when bad qualities may still help us when they are present in reasonable measures. Fear within reason will keep us safe ensuring that we don't foolishly jump into something dangerous.

Similarly, anger, desire and envy may sometime be useful.

But greed is like cyanide. Even a micro portion can inflict an irreparable damage.

Greedy people don't know when to back out of an investment or avoid a gamble.

Greed for applause will cause the focus to shift from actual performance. If the person does not receive the accolades (which he actually does not deserve as his focus was not on performance,) he sulks, develops anger, hatred, loses concentration, purity, honesty, ability to learn, intellect or the faculty to seek forgiveness, and finally perishes.

. . .

These 11 players in our mind cause over 180 confusions or cognitive biases.

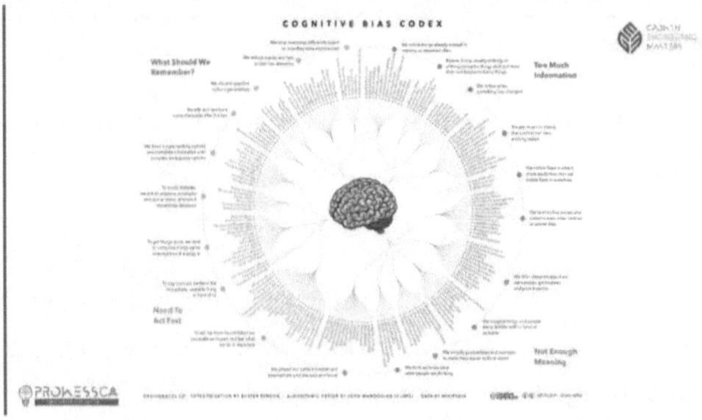

- Too much information
- Not enough meaning
- Need to act fast
- Prioritising information

A leader must ensure that he does not get into the trap of cognitive bias.

A quality control process is prone to two kinds of errors: Error of selecting a wrong item and the error of rejecting a right one. These are called type I and II errors.

A type II error could prove to be a costly mistake to a leader. Rejecting the right suggestion, initiative or person can derail the morale of team members and erode their confidence. They may come across as biased breeding trust and relationship issues.

. . .

Always validate all your assumptions and don't give any room for intelligence arrogance. Humility protects you.

RESISTANCE TWINS

Do you know that we have two monkeys inside our brains? They are called resistance twins.

The first one is in charge of the inner soul. He fights back whenever he sees something that can erode your values, reputation and purpose. Encourage him.

You keep seeing the second one more often. He is in charge of your body. He complains whenever your physical comforts are lost. Silence this guy. He is your only arch-rival. Fight and win the war every day. You will always lose if this guy wins.

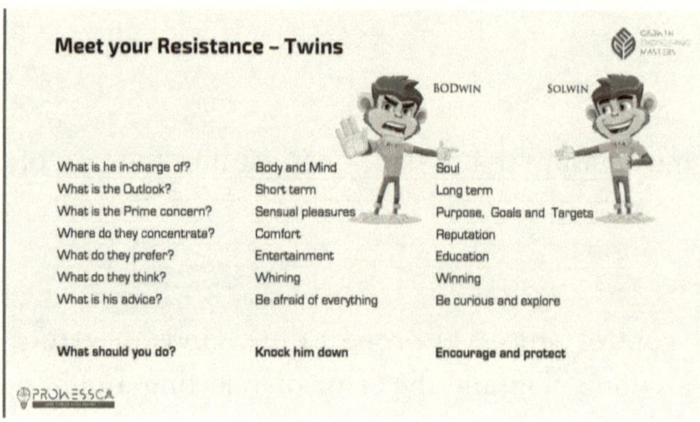

Let us name these twins Solwin (the one in charge of the soul) and Bodwin (the other one in charge of the body.)

LOCUS OF CONTROL

Ever wondered why two people react differently to the same situation or adversity?

When failure hits them, one asks, "Why is my fate bad all the time?" while the other ponders, "How can I improve it next time?"

Similarly, when they encounter an unpleasant situation at a workplace, one says, "Why is everyone against me?" while the other states, "What can I do better?"

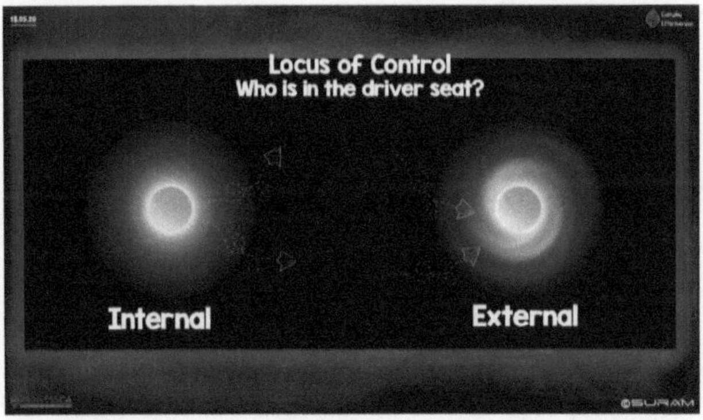

The list goes on.

We have something called the 'locus of control' in our mind. The locus comes in two forms: internal and external.

Persons with internal locus believe that they are responsible for their actions and control their destiny. They believe what happens is the ultimate result of their actions.

Whereas those with an external locus believe that fate controls their destiny and the whole world is attacking them.

What could be the OCEAN scores of these two people? Do you see any pattern?

RESILIENCE

We have studied the resistance twins and the locus of control. How do we ensure that Bodwin is silenced, and Solwin is encouraged?

How do we ensure that our 'locus of control' is positioned inside?

How do we find the strength to fight the internal evils?

Where do we draw our strength to fight all the adversities?

How do we develop all the ten virtues further?

Well, the answer to all these questions is by improving our resilience.

> "Resilience is a muscle. Flex it enough, and it will take less effort to get over the emotional punches each time."
>
> Alecia Moore

Resilience is our ability to bounce back from setbacks and failures.

Professor Peter Clough of Huddersfield University developed a model to improve mental toughness. It consists of four dimensions:

- Control
- Courage
- Commitment
- Challenge

The professor also collaborated with others to develop a Mental Toughness Questionnaire (MTQ.)

The questionnaire measures an individual's resilience and ability to cope with pressure and change the scales of challenge, control, commitment and confidence. The questionnaire is available online. It is well validated and takes approximately 15 minutes to complete.

As per the website, the development of MTQ Plus was led by Doug Strycharczyk supported by an elite academic team led by Prof. Peter Clough (Huddersfield University) and Dr John Perry (Hull University.)

Ancient Indian techniques to control the mind include yoga and meditation. There are various practices to alter the states of consciousness and achieve a great power of resilience.

. . .

Apart from conditioning the mind, these procedures also offer numerous health benefits.

As per the Indian system, we have three qualities of mind called *satva*, *tamasa* and *rajo*. They are called *trigunas*.

- *Satva* indicates mindfulness, calmness and harmony
- *Tamasa* points to passion, aggression, action and agility
- *Rajas* stands for anxiety, imbalance and negativity

Ancient saints were aware that everyone needed these qualities. Therefore, one's personality cannot be typecast. The composition of these three qualities should be balanced based on the profession, age, place, time and situation. The behaviour and treatment differ from person to person.

If a leader possesses only *satvic* qualities administration of duties will take a serious beating. Consider the following scenario:

- While dealing with planning and strategy, the leader needs to adopt a *satvic* mindset.
- While dealing with developmental activities, *tamo guna* needs to be demonstrated.
- Similarly, *rajo guna* is necessary while dealing with frauds and criminals.

The person who masters all ten qualities explained in the previous section, will also bring the 11 evils under control easily. Such a person will automatically acquire discretionary powers and wisdom.

The balance of these *gunas* are achieved through diet, pranayama and yoga. I will cover these in detail in my upcoming book. For now, think of pranayama as a controlled and rhythmic breathing activity.

Vedic scriptures have also laid out detailed procedures and principles that may be employed to judge situations and persons in an unbiased manner. While they are spread across various manuscripts, they are specifically mentioned in three philosophical branches called *Nyaya, Tarka* and *Vaisheshika.*

Whichever method you adopt, it is essential to inculcate the ten virtues and conquer the eleven evils. It all starts from there.

SKILL VS. SENSE

As we explore our minds and master the virtues, we need to take up continuous learning. To stay focused on our objective and to accelerate our learning, we need to acquire several skills, develop senses and set standards.

To do it effectively, we need to understand the subtle difference between a skill and a sense.

> "Skill is about successfully winning an argument with your boss. Sense lies in not even attempting it."
>
> Suram

Let's consider communication skills. Many people in this world have excellent communication skills. However, are all of them successful? Not really. People fail despite their ability to communicate. Why? They lack the essence or the communication sense.

You need to differentiate between skill and sense. You can learn many skills, but if you lack the discretion to use those, you will soon become a menace. Let's take a few examples:

As you walk across the road, you will notice many drivers on vehicles. Chances are over 99 percent of them hold a valid license. That means they may be reasonably skilled in driving. However, is it sufficient?

What about the other critical essentials?

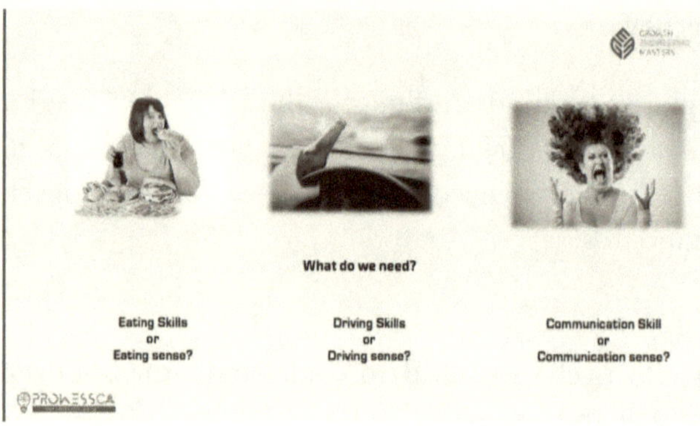

Civic Sense: To avoid drinking and driving, using mobile phones, controlling emissions from the vehicle, refraining from playing loud music and concentrating on the road.

Traffic sense: To follow traffic rules, avoiding honking, staying in the lane, controlling the speed and complying with the rules.

Other senses: Community sense, sense of the terrain, sense of direction, and many more.

What happens when a skilled driver with zero percent sense drives near a school zone? It may turn into an act of terror.

In discreet and senseless people are omnipresent menaces. Like mosquitoes, they suck blood and inject stress.

Did you ever hear anyone saying "I have excellent eating skills" You don't need eating skills. You need eating sense.

Obesity rates are soaring over 35 percent and another 30 percent are fast turning corpulent. Essentially, 70 percent of the population only possess eating skills.

These figures are in fact heartening if you pit them against those for communication sense.

Communication sense is both about communicating with the inner self and the external world. You need to establish a communication channel with your inner self and route all communications with the outer world through the same.

OPPORTUNITY ZONES

Many a time, as we learn a particular skill and practice it, we start getting positive vibes from the external world. People start praising and flattering us. Over time, we end up with the sense that we have mastered the subject, and there is hardly anything left to learn further. This brings in complacency. That is the starting point of impotence.

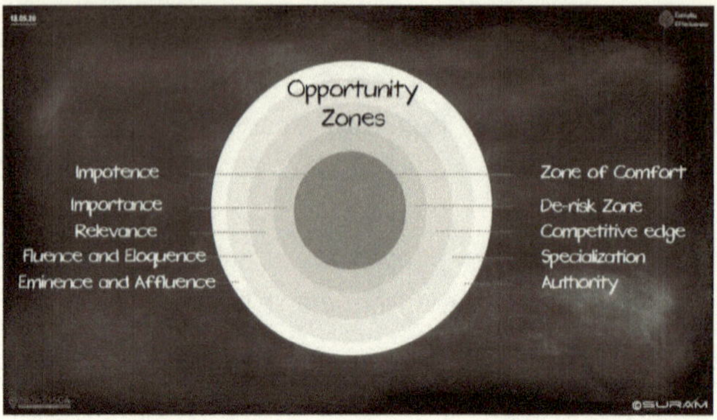

Let's look at the centre of the comfort zone. We have accomplished things and feel proud. But after a while, several new skills and fresh methods of executing things will crop up. There is no shortcut to bridge the gap. We need to learn and expand our comfort zones continually.

- At the core is our comfort zone.
- Expand it a bit and you will move to a de-risked zone. Temporary changes will no longer challenge you.
- Move a bit more, and you will move to a competitive zone. You transform into an accomplished person.
- Move on. You will get to a specialisation zone. The world will reckon you are an expert and there will be very few people like you. You will be confident in what you do. You will earn eloquence.
- Explore further and you will become an authority in your subject. You will find eminence and affluence. You will become synonymous with your subject matter. Your reputation starts shining.

- You need to move and expand your base progressively. Otherwise, your comfort zone will shrink by the day and you will become completely irrelevant.

Which of your comfort zones do you need to expand?

- VIA character strengths
- Deeper exploration of talent strengths and signature themes
- Your resilience scores
- Your core quotients (CQ, EQ, DQ, and IQ)
- Skills that help you manage the external environment (Chapter 4)
- Top future skills and highest-paid skills (Chapter 5)
- Improve OCEA and decrease the N in OCEAN

How to expand your comfort zone?

Moving from impotence to eminence:

- You need to have the **ambition** to be unique and relevant
- Nurture the **belief** that you need to expand your comfort zone and that you have the ability and environment to do so
- Obtain **clarity** about the depth of the subject and prioritise
- Cultivate the **discipline** to pursue a new topic until you master it

You might say, "Cultivating an ABCD mindset is fine but how do I conquer my fears?"

Let us see what we can do about the fear factors.

T-SHAPED LEADER

There is a concept of T-shaped leader popularised by Tim Brown, the co-founder of IDEO, a design and innovation company.

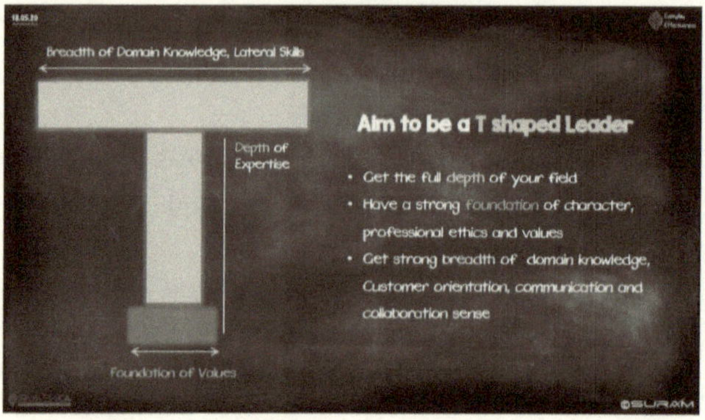

The T-shaped leader is one who has breadth of the domain knowledge, the lateral skills and depth of expertise.

I would also recommend you to add a foundation layer of character values to this.

- Understand the full depth of your field.
- Build a strong foundation of character, professional ethics and values.
- Acquire a strong breadth of domain knowledge, customer orientation, communication and collaboration.

David Clifford, the founder of Design School X outlines the X-shaped leader who comes with leadership and technical skills. However, I feel that it is essential to become T-shaped leader first.

CONQUERING FEAR

> "It is not what you achieve. It's what you overcome. That's what defines your career."
>
> - Carlton Fisk

Are you SAD (experience Stress, Anxiety, and Depression?)

Do you suffer from FUD (Fear, Uncertainty, and Doubt) fatigue? You are not alone.

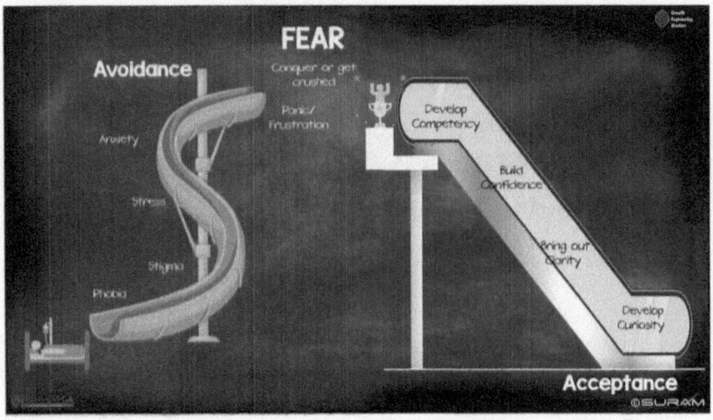

Fear is often what comes your way when you want to move out of your comfort zone. Let's see what fear is all about and how to conquer it.

. . .

We are not talking about staying fearless while doing something illegal and unethical.

We are talking about the fears you may have developed that are controlling a large part of your life.

For some people, fear might work as a stimulant. If you are not afraid of your boss, you may not stick to the timelines. But it's not something that needs to be controlled or stimulated by fear.

You need to develop discipline and strengthen your values to avoid making such mistakes.

The point is to be a bit sceptical to avoid being taken in by situations.

If you accept the challenge and are prepared to conquer, you will be stepping on the escalator.

- You will develop curiosity
- You will bring clarity
- You will build confidence
- You will develop competency
- You will finally conquer fear

On the contrary, if you avoid the challenge:

- You will never get out of panic situations
- You will breed anxiety
- Become stressed

- Be stigmatised
- Develop a phobia

There is a problem if you are avoiding activities you are expected to do to prosper. It will foment anxiety, stress, frustration and tons of negativity. Sometimes fear can manifest as hatred or phobia in certain situations. Some of these might require psychiatric interventions.

How to work on your fears?

CALM down and conquer your fears

- **Compose** yourself
- **Accept** the challenge
- **Learn** the secrets
- **Master** the subject

Compose yourself and give an auto command that it is high time you overcame the fear of doing something.

Picture all the positive things that will happen to you once you overcome the fear. It could be a fear of public speaking, fear of failure and the like.

Observe your colleagues or competitors in a similar situation. Find out the tricks of the trade. Practice, practice and practice!

Sachin Tendulkar, the god of Indian cricket, once said, "I have converted all stones pelted at me to milestones."

Those who make failure their stepping stones will never fall.

Sometimes, you need to think out-of-the-box to knock off your opponent and fear at the same time. You need to develop the mindset.

- **Ambition**. Overcome fear. It is your turn to scare others
- **Believe** that you have the need and support to conquer fear
- **Clarity** about the fear and how others deal with similar situations
- **Discipline** to chase fear until you win against it
- Follow the **CALM** method

You can apply the above method to any of these common fears.

- Speaking in English (If English is not your native language)
- Making a presentation
- Public speaking
- Report writing
- Interacting with strangers
- Persuading team members
- Negotiation
- Conflict resolution

You need to be passionate about conquering your fears. When you demonstrate perseverance, you will come up with innovative ideas to help you.

Let me tell you the story of a gentleman who conquered the fear in the most innovative way.

CLASH OF THE TITANS

Master stroke vs. master strategy

In the 80s the German tennis player Boris Becker was unstoppable. He never used to allow the opponent to even serve. Boris would serve and smash the opponent. He played against American champion Andre Agassi and crushed him in all the matches.

While Andre's coaches were helping him with different methods to counter Boris, Andre felt that he needed a different strategy. He wanted to observe Boris' playing style carefully and understand his approach and shortcomings. So, Andre left everything and watched all his match videos relentlessly. Those close to Andre did not understand his strategy and felt that he had gone nuts.

After watching several matches of Boris, Andre identified a pattern. Every time Boris served the ball, he had a habit of sticking his tongue out. He also noticed another systematic pattern. If his tongue was straight, the ball would land in the middle of the court. If it went to a corner, the ball was being served wide. That was the turning point for Andre. Out of the 11 matches he played with Becker, Andre had nine victories. He emerged a hero at the Wimbledon and the US Open.

After both had retired and when they met, Boris asked him about the secret. Andre revealed what he had learned. Boris was stunned and said, "I used to go home to my wife and tell her, 'It's like he reads my mind!' Now I understand you were reading my tongue!"

So, sometimes, you need innovative thinking and will power to overcome the weakness. Had Andre developed fear, America would have lost nine matches.

4T MODEL OF RISK MANAGEMENT

Fears are risks. We have a famous risk management model to combat threats.

Identify your shortcomings and follow the 4T approach to mitigate them.

- Terminate: Work on fear and conquer.
- Treat: Work on minor issues.
- Transfer: Identify a team member who can complement you.
- Tolerate: Live with the residual risk (not recommended.)

Remember, you need to work with your team members and take up this activity for all your teammates.

You need to decide whether you want to belong to the pack of rats or pride of lions.

If you have one or more irrational fears, you will be called a rat in a pack. If you help each other and plug the loophole, you will be a lions in a pride.

MOTIVATION TYPES

There are different ways to find motivation. Each of us will have our reasons to self-motivate.

. . .

Depending on the underlying factors, scientists have categorised them into two types:

- Intrinsic goals
- Extrinsic goals

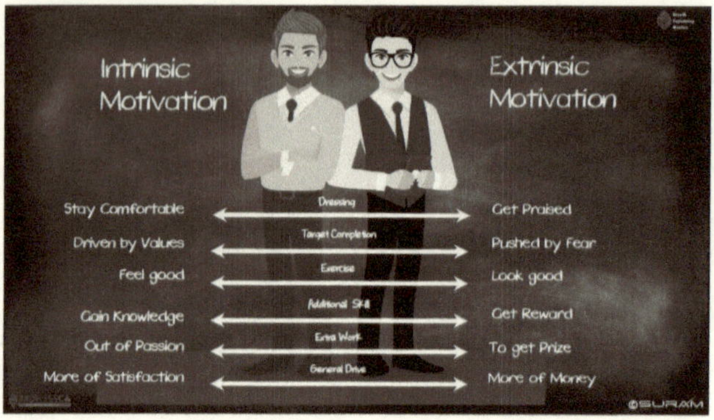

If you observe the picture above, you will notice a steady pattern. Although the goals are the same, the underlying reasons for motivation are entirely different.

Broadly, extrinsic goals change, intrinsic goals remain permanent. When you identify your own inner strengths and that of your team's, you will form a shared vision. This is explained in detail by two famous psychologists and research scientists Edward Deci and Richard Ryan in their theory : The self-determination theory.

This theory explains three primary intrinsic needs that underpin our self-determination and motivation: autonomy, competence, and relatedness.

Accept that adversity is your teacher.

. . .

Warren Buffett (An American business tycoon and one of the most successful investors on the planet) once said "Making money isn't the backbone of our guiding purpose; making money is the by-product of our guiding purpose. If you're doing something you love, you're more likely to put your all into it, and that generally equates to making money."

GOAL-SETTING

Now that we have understood the components of the mind positioning system we need to set meaningful goals.

SWOT and SOAR analyses will give us an excellent start in identifying the current gaps. Please fill these up in the context of your current goals.

SOAR

Strengths:

- List your strengths (we discussed in the previous section)
- Skills you believe you have
- Signature themes as per Clifton
- VIA character Skills

Opportunities

- Improvement areas
- Feedback from colleagues and clients

- Gaps in VIA character skills
- Gaps in the four quotients

Aspirations

- What do you want to become?

Results

- Which metrics indicate progress and goal attainment?
- You can download the template from http://gem.prowessca.com.
- Once you do it, you need to adopt a structured method to pursue your goals.

GOAL-SETTING | GET YOUR GRIT

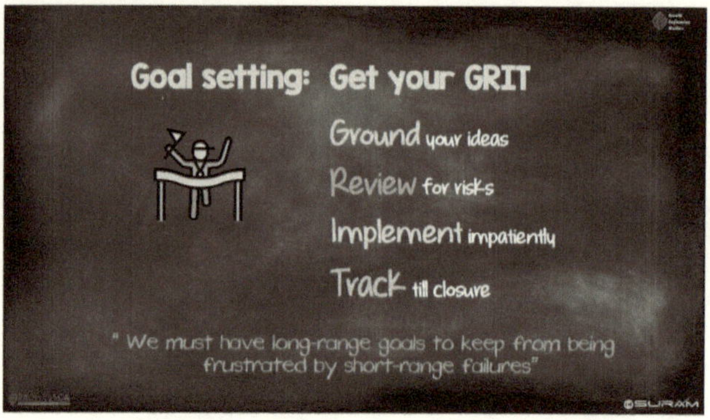

- Ground your ideas
- Review for risks
- Implement them impatiently

- Track until closure

Ground your ideas

There is a difference between ideas flying and ideas in the air.

When ideas are in the air, they are called superficial and impractical. When you ground them and validate the practicality and execute them, they are called ideas flying.

When you set specific, measurable, achievable, realistic, and time-bound (SMART) goals you can ground your ideas. We will examine how we can root your ideas without a grind. We'll talk about this later in the chapter.

Review risks

Identify all possible obstacles that can delay or derail your implementation. Some of them include

- Lack of focus or inability to spend adequate time
- Family and workplace obligations
- Skill gaps
- Wrong prioritisation
- Wrong goals

Implement and track

. . .

In the following sections, we will see what the different types of goals are and which of them are better. We will understand the risk management framework and will apply it to each of our goals. We will also learn about how to build a team and create a shared vision. Finally, we will look at various delegation techniques and tracking tools.

We will revisit this topic in the last section and will try to set meaningful short-term and long-term goals.

BALANCED SUPPORT SYSTEM

You always seek support from those around you. How much help do you get from your body and mind every day? Do you have healthy habits that take you closer to your goals? Did your mind permit you to set a meaningful goal yet?

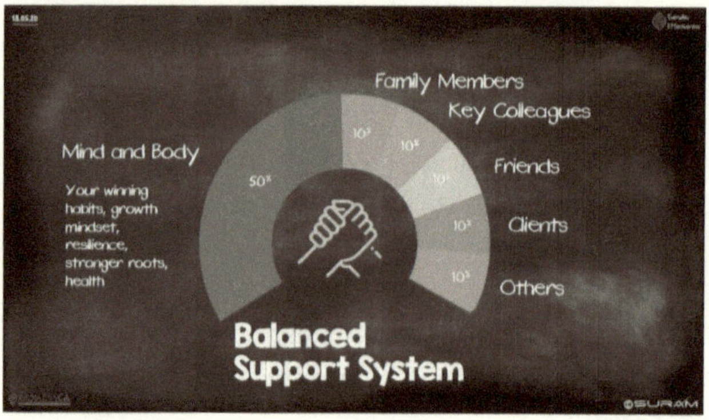

As you step back and analyse, you will realise that the majority of transformation should happen from within. Our body and mind should support us with winning habits.

. . .

• We need to master a method to silence Bodwin and encourage Solwin.

- We can work on our fears on our own.
- We can move out of the comfort zone ingeniously.
- We can develop the resilience to fight.
- We can align our locus of control and build stronger roots.

We don't need the support of anyone to do all these. Once you understand this, you will become self-reliant and self-sufficient.

Then we can use the external support sparingly for our personal or professional development. External support will help us maximise group efforts on team goals.

SUMMARY

This brings us to the end of this chapter. We have learnt the following :

- Self-awareness is the key to our success
- Our Mind Positioning System, though basic, will navigate us successfully
- We can adjust the locus of control with some effort
- We need to silence the resistance monkey
- Character is the fundamental pillar of our growth
- VIA character test helps us identify 24-character strengths
- The Big Five personality test assesses our openness, conscientiousness, extroversion, agreeability and neuroticism
- We need to identify our strengths and play to them. Clifton Strengths test lists the required signature strength themes

- We need to follow a 4 T approach to minimise our shortcomings
- Self-help is the best help
- By using a structured approach, we will be in a position to conquer our fears and overcome greed
- Intrinsic motivation is the key to setting long-term, sustainable and meaningful goals
- We need to show the grit to follow the GRIT
- SWOT and SOAR will help us profile our plans better
- Mental toughness is a muscle exercise
- It is critical to develop your sense in addition to skills
- Developing the ten virtues will effortlessly take us closer to success
- Snubbing the eleven evils will smoothen our journey
- Moving out of the comfort zone is critical for our career success

We will now move to fourth chapter. In Fourth chapter, we will cover the environmental quotient end to end. This is the longest chapter and contains many practical tools and techniques. Buckle up!

4

EXTERNAL WORLD

Om Saha Nau-Avatu |
Saha Nau Bhunaktu |
Saha Viiryam Karavaavahai |
Tejasvi Nau-Adhiitam-Astu Maa Vidvissaavahai |
Om Shaantih Shaantih Shaantih | |

Aum! May he protect us both together;
may he nourish us both together;
May we work conjointly with great energy,
May our study be vigorous and effective;

May we not mutually dispute (or may we not hate anyone).
Aum! Let there be peace in me.
Let there be peace in my environment.
Let there be peace in the forces that act on me.

IN THE LAST CHAPTER, we learned self-management, ways to control the mind and about the several evil deterrents.

. . .

All of those will come in handy when we deal with the external world. By being conscious of our external dealings, we can enhance the first four qualities of OCEAN and minimise or eliminate the last one.

LEARNING OBJECTIVES

At the end of this session, you will be able to

- Understand the criticality of communication skills
- Appreciate the requirement of classifying various stakeholders and nurturing relationships
- Devise a structured approach for communication in multiple scenarios
- Appreciate the need for profiling teams and tasks
- Understand the proven methods to prioritise projects, gauge the depth and set expectations
- Follow a structured path to achieve client satisfaction
- Learn the secrets of
- Presentation sense
- Negotiation
- Motivation
- Persuasion
- Conflict resolution

MICRO EVENTS AT THE WORKPLACE

The following might sound trivial and obvious but over 90 percent of employees get this wrong.

At the workplace, we need to handle multiple micro events:

- One-on-one emails
- Group emails
- One-on-one phone calls
- Audio and video conferences
- Face-to-face meetings with the team
- Face-to-face meetings with clients or supervisor
- Other team meetings
- Messaging and using social media
- Project management

Each situation demands a different strategy, etiquette, engagement, sense of context and terrain. Once we are aware of the purpose and are conscious of the expectations, we can be better prepared to handle the event.

Just the way you treat a party or ceremony as an event, you need to look at each of these as events. No doubt they are micro events, but critical even so. Sometimes they could be vital and life-changing.

So, you need to be conscious of these micro events and plan adequately. If you attend these events in a casual or a semi-conscious way, it will not help the cause.

The higher the consciousness levels, the more sensitive and responsive you become

Mindfulness pushes you to plan and execute better. While trying to accomplish better things, you will become more open, conscientious, agreeable and extroverted. Similarly, your neuroticism levels will also come down pushing you closer to success and eminence.

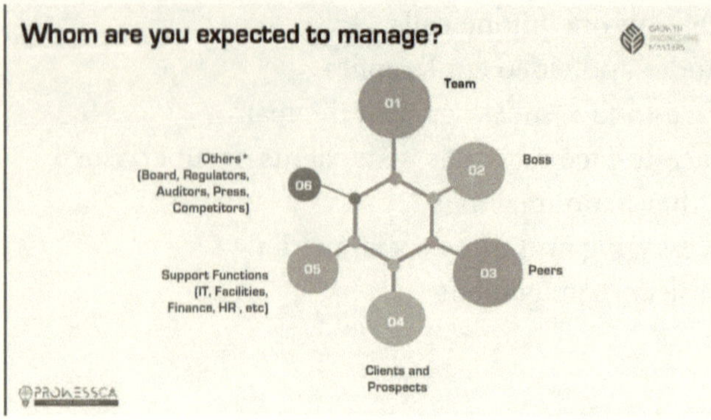

In our day to day life, who are we expected to manage?

- Team members
- Boss
- Peers
- Clients
- Prospects
- Various support functions like IT, facilities, finance and HR
- Depending on designation and job function some may need to deal with competitors, auditors, press, board members and even regulators

We are covering only workplace relationships, consciously excluding the ones at the home front.

. . .

Managing better relationships with them will have a host of benefits like improved productivity, better engagement, stronger empathy, healthier bonds and enhanced charisma.

> "The single biggest problem in communication is the illusion that it has taken place."
>
> George Bernard Shaw

What are we expected to manage?

We need to

- Manage the delivery
- Improve relationships
- Minimise conflicts
- Handle negotiations
- Persuade and motivate people
- Handle exceptions

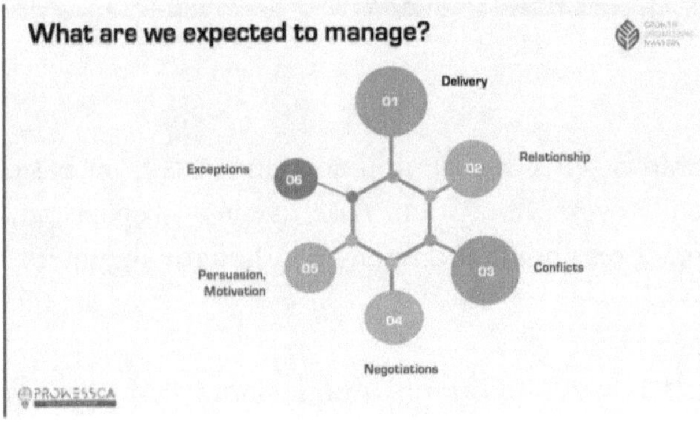

Almost all of them need proactive management and careful sensing to save them from turning into a crisis.

The efficient handling of these situations provides an excellent opportunity to prove our mettle and improve our relationships at the workplace. If not handled well, this can result in conflicts and permanent scars on the relationship. Daily expectation management is the key to fostering relationships.

Out of all the skills and senses we learn, communication is the most crucial and powerful one. The following is a pyramid of effective communication. In this chapter, we will cover each of these topics.

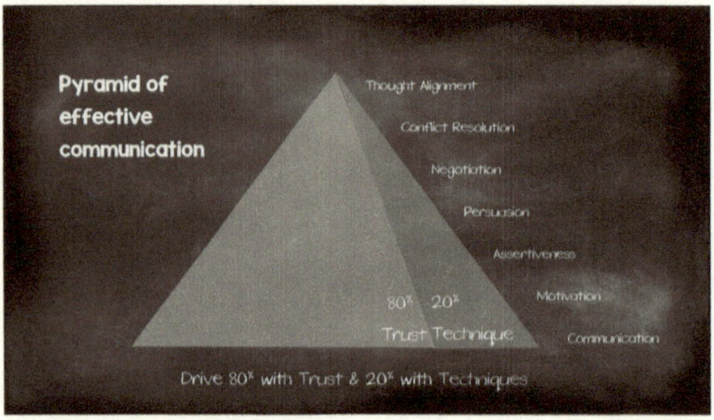

The pyramid of effective communication starts from basic communication and covers Motivation, Assertiveness , Persuasion, Negotiation , Conflict resolution and finally the thought alignment.

However, It Is very important to understand that we drive 80% of our point by being trustworthy. All other tools and techniques contribute only 20%.

. . .

But before we delve into these topics, we will cover presentation sense and skills. Presentation skill lays a structural and sound foundation for learning the other skills.

Presentation sense

In this section, we are going to cover the presentation skills and senses. We chose presentation sense as the first topic in our external communication series.

This because an effective presentation has a fine blend of all other communication skills. It takes a whole lot of collaboration, motivation, persuasion, conflict resolution, assertiveness to put together a persuasive presentation.

At the end of this session, you should be able to

- Understand why presentation sense is essential for your career growth
- Appreciate various tools and techniques to craft a compelling presentation
- Identify top mistakes that even pros make and understand how to correct them
- Apply content to the context
- Create persuasive presentations for any occasion using a structured and time-tested approach

> "There are always three speeches for everyone you gave. The one you practiced, the one you gave, and the one you wish you gave."
>
> Dale Carnegie

There are widespread notions and criticisms about the utility of presentation tools particularly, PowerPoint. No matter what anyone feels, the need to present an idea is strongly embedded. Misconceptions prevailed as unskilled people misused the tool and blamed the outcome on the application.

More than 30 million PowerPoint presentations are made each day. Communication and presentation skills are deemed to be the top make or break skills across the globe.

Most people think that creating a presentation is all about opening PowerPoint and copying all their old documents into it. Some people enhance the presentation using their skills. They use dazzling colours, insert animations and reduce an entire document into a single slide. Others go a bit too far. They animate each letter adding a typewriter sound effect.

Trust me. No one is interested in your talent show. People who have imbalanced PowerPoint skill and sense may be eager to demonstrate their animation skills subjecting audiences to a boring and uninspiring experience.

. . .

In the whole presentation crafting experience, PowerPoint plays only a five percent role. The concentration should be on the design. Design elements include content, context, and clarity.

At this juncture, you may ask, if we divert 85 percent of our efforts into designing what about the rest?

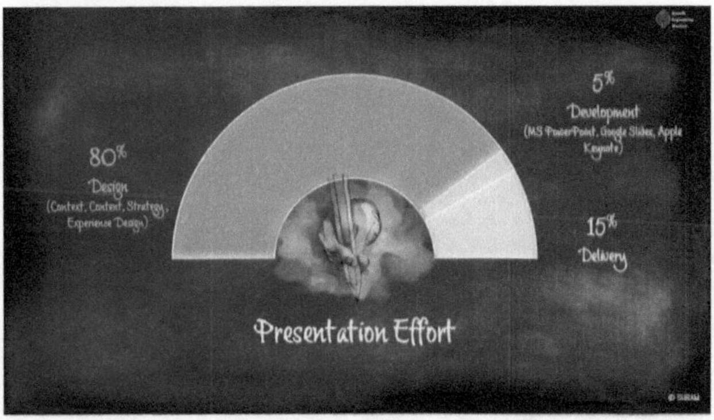

Presentation development: Thanks to online marketplaces and content-sharing platforms, there is no shortage of designer slides available online. Thanks to the growing gig economy and freelancing, you also need not worry about PowerPoint skills. If you know what needs to be done, there are hundreds of professionals whose help you can enlist. What is difficult is injecting the sense into it. We will review various online platforms during the latter part of this session.

Presentation delivery: You are designing an experience. We will exclusively focus on the design aspects in this section. A thoughtfully and tastefully crafted presentation is easy on the brain and appealing to the heart. It is a pleasant experience for the presenter and the audience.

. . .

Usually, managers worry about presenting something to their audience. They experience fear and anxiety or even have nightmares. However, studies indicate that it's the audience that worries even more.

Most people in the corporate world have a tendency to repurpose and recycle presentations.

For example, they may revise an induction presentation to a show a business prospect.

Invariably, they end up presenting something irrelevant to the audience. What do we call this?

Committing a severe corporate crime by taking the audience close to death!

The punishment term could extend from an hour to a whole day. I am discounting the aftershock the audience suffers after the session.

Depending on the situation, it can prove to be very costly to the organisation.

How do we know if you have committed such corporate crimes in the past?

. . .

Well, take a look at your last presentation deck and ask yourself the following questions. Rate each aspect of your presentation on a scale of 1 to 10. Give one for the worst and give ten for the best.

- The content presented is entirely relevant to the intended subject or solution. (Weightage: 2)
- For example, you showed an induction presentation at a business meet. ((Weightage:1)
- The content thoroughly holds the listeners' interest and is contextual. They are interested in only one point: What is in it for me? ((Weightage:1)
- The claims you have made and items you have listed were fully measurable and verifiable. ((Weightage:1)
- For example, did you make abstract statements like "We have a huge clientele list;" "We have a mass following;" We are the largest..." or "Our customers love us?" ((Weightage:1)
- Each slide has a purpose and a prime takeaway. (*The primary objective of the presentation and the underlying message is loud and clear.)* ((Weightage:1)
- For example, stating the benefits rather than extolling the features. Mentioning the fine-print, resource utilisation in terms of money, people and time. ((Weightage:1)
- The overall presentation is easy on the eye and brain. ((Weightage:3)

Reduce a point each for non-compliance of the last item (The overall presentation is easy on the eye and brain)

- Use of jargons
- Excessive use of similar phrases, adjectives and repetitions
- Ambiguous expressions

- Font size lesser than 14
- Rainbow colours
- Excessive animations (cut ten marks for each animation)
- Sound effects for animations
- Unformatted numbers
- Large paragraphs or more than 10 bullet points
- Other innovative ideas that may be confusing to the audience

Summing up:

- The content stays within the purview of the subject
- It holds the interests of the audience
- Each statement, fact or claim made is completely measurable
- Suggestions given in slides were practical and objective
- All messages packed in bullets are loud and clear
- The overall presentation is eye catching and easy to assimilate

Finally, is your presentation simple enough? You will know in a minute.

- Multiply your ratings with the weightage points for each question. Total your score.
- Request a member of the audience who sat through your presentation (it could be your friend, client, boss, peer or subordinate) for feedback.
- How did they rank you? If you could not get a score from them for whatever reason, no problem. How do you think they will rate you? We are not going to publish

the results on your facebook wall, so be honest and mention the correct score.
- Subtract your score from theirs. This is your Gap.

Gap

- Revenue or monetary Impact. Keep the gap <5
- Relationship building. Keep the gap <5
- Matters concerning the interests of the organisation, customer, family or nation. <5
- New concept or idea. <10
- Any other presentation <10

What has caused this gap, and how do I bridge this?

The gap could have occurred due to lack of ideas or your incapacity to express them. Whatever be the issue, this condition is called 'thought-constipation.' Everyone experiences it to some degree and it is entirely curable. A mild constipation could cause a minor bottleneck. Severe constipation emits toxins and can become a hindrance to your success. We will address the issue of thought-constipation. In this section, we will check your current thought-constipation level. Remember, every person suffers from it to a certain extent. It could be because of lousy consumption habits or poor intake of dietary fibre which translates to absence of good content and poor judgement of the context.

Given below is a list of questions. You need to respond with a yes or no. Give yourself a mark for each yes.

- I find it difficult to express my ideas.
- I realise that I often assume others understand what I mean.
- People seem to understand my viewpoint after they have experienced it themselves and not when I explain it to them.
- People often tell me, "You did not come across that way."
- Most of our prospective clients don't respond to my calls after I finish my presentations.
- I know that my presentation looks outdated, but I don't know how to improve it.
- I always want to explain things better but I fail miserably.
- I envy people with excellent communication and presentation skills.
- I could have done better in my career if I were a bit more proficient in presentation.
- I always struggle to explain my ideas to my friends and colleagues. My boss trashes most of them.
- I want to try a new initiative that can transform my workplace, but I don't know how to initiate a discussion on it.
- The application I use at the office sucks. I have a few ideas on improving the user interface but I do not know how to explain it to the IT team.
- We have created a great product but none of our prospective clients seem interested.
- We have built great products and services but our customers and prospects always undervalue them.
- We waste a lot of time making changes to our business applications. The amount of work after each review is killing productivity and costing time, money and enthusiasm.
- Enhancing my presentation skills will help me achieve higher productivity and effectiveness.

- I need to pick up some essential persuasion skills before I get promoted or give way to my peers and juniors who have better presentation skills.
- I keep looking for help frantically in all directions but God does not seem to give me a hand in this area alone.

Please visit the assessments section of gem.prowessca.com and take an online assessment. If you have scored above 95, congratulations! You are passionate about your work, and you are clear about your objectives. I am sure you will find this chapter refreshing. If you have scored between 70 and 95 percent; you are almost there but your approach may need a little bit of tweaking. This chapter is all about fine-tuning your innate talents. Scored less than 70 percent? Do not worry. By the end of this chapter, you will master the presentation skills you need.

Remember, it pays to sharpen the saw.

Buying buttons inside our brains

Let's look at the buying buttons in our brains. There are three main parts to our minds. The right brain controls thinking, logic and rationality. The left-brain controls feelings and emotions. The middle brain, which is also called the reptilian brain is responsible for making decisions subconsciously. As this is the part that we have inherited from the reptiles and other early creatures, this part of the brain knows only three things: fight, flight, and freeze. It fights when it senses the enemy approaching and runs away or freezes when it senses danger. Therefore, the natural reaction of the brain is to supply blood to the legs and hands. This seriously deprives the brain of the blood and oxygen to think. If you are left with only a few drops of blood in your brain, you will only end up making funny gestures and silly sounds.

. . .

The subconscious mind makes 95 percent of our decisions. The subconscious mind controls essential aspects such as

- Beliefs
- Emotions
- Habits
- Imagination
- Intuition

So, if we appeal to our subconscious brain, a large chunk of our work is done. This brain does not like too much fodder. If you overload it with too many things, it will deliver nothing.

You have to package the information as if you are feeding an infant. Remember the following characteristics of the brains:

- They do not come with hunger sensors
- They are always on diet mode
- They can remember and register only four items at once
- They wander 30 percent of the time
- They can only learn in 20 minute chunks or less
- Memory takes up a lot of mental resources

Triggering the URGE

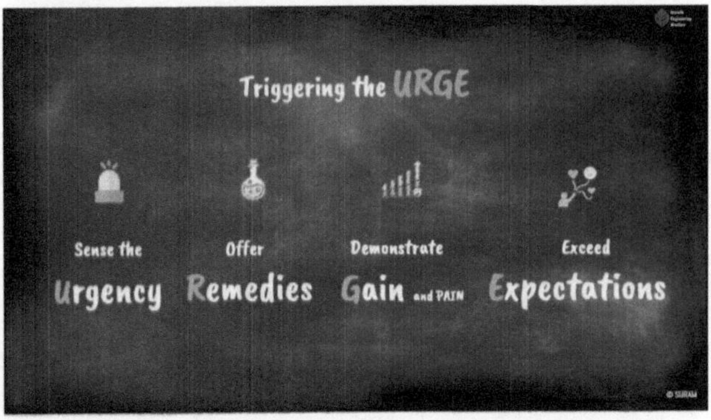

Whether it is a large project or small product, you need to create an urge in the customer's mind to accept it. Most of the gadgets we own today are results of such an irrational urge.

The same is true even for a movie, stage show or a presentation. You need to create the urge for them to ask for more

- **Understand** the situation
- Offer **remedies**
- Demonstrate the **gain** (in accepting your solution) and the pain (in rejecting it)
- Build **excitement**

Does your presentation create the URGE?

Do you have a complete understanding of the environment, possible remedies, gains of your solution, and pains if the client rejects or postpones?

Preparation

"The will to win is important. But the will to prepare is vital."

Joe Paterno

Brush up or rush in? Outstanding presentations require extraordinary preparation.

The presentation development stage is the right time to strategise and think about the best possible way to market your product, idea or solution.

Opting for shortcuts in this area can seriously undermine the quality of your product offerings. If you have built something with passion, you need to present it with passion.

Let's assume that you are launching a new company or a product. You are confident that the product you are going to sell indeed offers extraordinary value to your customers.

- Your product is ready.
- You hire a creative agency, and they come up with a brilliant video, and some audio and billboard advertisements.
- Your entire team worked hard and exhibited all-round brilliance.
- Now, the first customer walks into your office for a 30-

minute presentation before he decides to sign up for a large order.

What do most people do in this situation?

- Some show product brochures.
- Some show them TV commercials.
- Some read out radio advertisements.
- Some go a step forward by making a fat presentation on the company's history, product evolution detailing how they failed at every stage before finally becoming successful.

This is not what your prospect expected to see. What will be the price of this last-minute botch up?

Yes, serious presentations require equally serious commitment. Look at these mountains and massive rock formations.

Now, look at these carvings:

These are precious monolithic carvings found in Indian temples. Before they were transformed into such beautiful carvings, they were massive rocks.

Such intricate and mesmerising carvings were accomplished by a pair of hands and a set of tools. Remember, there was no machinery involved. There were probably no blueprints and most importantly, no 'undo' and 'redo' options.

It takes enormous imagination, passion, perseverance, and talent to create such carvings. We need just nanobytes of these to create our slides. But there is one more critical aspect behind these great works. The process. What was the process adopted by them? They took a large block of stone and removed the unnecessary portions. The part thus left behind is what we admire.

Can we not adopt this process of elimination or editing to create an exciting slide or presentation? Yes, we can, if we have our ABCDs in place.

Aspiration

- To deliver a successful presentation
- Win the mandate

Belief

- We can deliver an excellent presentation
- We don't know much about the participants and their expectations
- We have to correct the wrong notions they may have about our products or services
- What we have so far may not take us there. We need to do substantial homework.

Clarity

- We need to create a questionnaire to get structured inputs
- We need to validate our content development and presentation delivery methods

Discipline

- We need to carry out dress rehearsals
- We need to continue to practice until we are perfect
- We are prepared to sacrifice a few things for a much higher gratification rewarded by victory

Making the whole thing SIMPLE

The temptation to pack in as much information as possible can undermine the person who is creating a presentation.

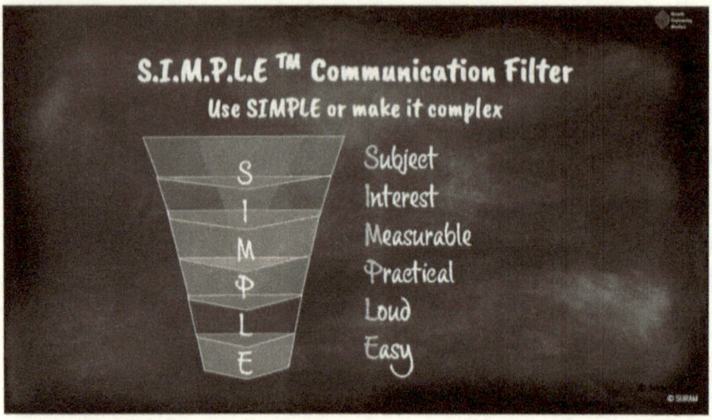

You think PowerPoint. The audience thinks pressure point. The SIMPLE filter is what transforms it from a pressure point to a pleasure point. We need to make sure that our slideshow does not end up as a horror show. To transform our slideshow into a magic show, we have a special six-stage filter called SIMPLE.

- Keep it relevant to the current **subject or solution**
- Covers listeners' **interest** and context
- Make only **measurable** statements and claims
- Keep it **practical** and palatable
- Ensure all messages are **loud** and **clear**
- Make sure it is **easy** on the eye and the mind

Subject orientation

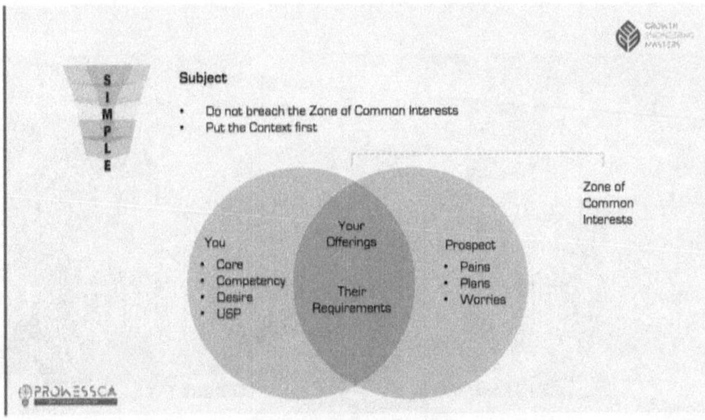

What is a subject? It is an idea or a concept that you want to sell to your colleagues or teammates. It could also be a solution, product or service that you are marketing to your prospective customers. Draw a boundary line and make sure that the content stays within that space.

Each slide should contain references to the solution that the prospect is looking for. While it is incredibly tempting to showcase everything that we have, the prospect may not be interested in looking at all of them at once. By packing in too much, we are only diluting the main message.

Every slide should directly or indirectly strengthen the case in hand, that is, the solution we are providing or the problem that we are solving. If the topics we present do not refer to this central theme, then they are redundant. If the client finds your statements to be sensible, he or she will instantly acknowledge them unless they want to purposefully hold back the appreciation. The acknowledgement could be through body language or verbal statements. The client may then engage in a discussion post presentation.

. . .

Remember, if content is the king, context is the king maker.

Your context could be anything that falls within the zone of common interest. If you move out of this, you will find it challenging to come back.

How do we find the context?

Let us assume that we are expecting a very valuable prospect to visit our office and evaluate our products and services. A successful presentation will convert them to a prestigious client. This is our context. Therefore, we need to ask all the relevant questions pertaining to this context. We need to do precise participant profiling to understand the complete details of the participants.

- What are the stakes?
- What is the delegate or participant profile?
- What is the path that they are likely to take?
- What is the path that we want them to take?
- Are we on the same page?

- Do we have that AAA (Triple-A) rated person in the group?
- What are the questions that we need to ask them?
- What do we expect from them towards the end of the journey?

Setting the right path for your project is the most critical aspect of the whole journey. A job well begun is half done. At this stage, we have to find answers to a lot of questions. The more answers we have, the fewer the surprises. Try to respond to each of the following questions to obtain full clarity on the subject. You will be surprised to see how many details you had missed before this activity.

What are the stakes involved? (How important is this presentation to you or your organisation?)

This is by far the most important question. This question determines what you will win and what you are likely to lose, depending on whether the final pitch is successful or not.

The higher the stakes, the greater the number of hours of preparation needed involving more team members.

What is the duration of presentation? (The number of slides and placement of images should be determined by the duration)

Knowing the duration in advance will help you plan and sequence the steps in advance and space the key aspects uniformly across the presentation. Ensure that there is no room to commit another corporate crime again.

To the extent possible, ensure that:

- The presentation time does not exceed twenty minutes at a single stretch
- The number of slides is capped at twenty
- You factor in an hour of preparation time for each slide

How large is the presentation room? (We need to apply the colours and font sizes accordingly)

How many participants will attend? (Exclude the members from your team)

Who are all likely to attend this presentation?

- AAA Rated Person*
- Key people
- Opinion makers
- Trouble maker
- Brand ambassador
- Fence sitter
- Other neutral participants

Who is a **AAA Rated Person?**

While making investments, we always check the the stock or bond to make sure that it has the highest rating or the AAA rating.

Similarly, we need to employ a similar strategy to deal with the person with the AAA rating. You can identify them based on following attributes:

- Appetite
- Affordability
- Authority

This person may or may not have the need, but if they have the appetite for our solution, it is sufficient for making our pitch. If you are not convinced, take a look at your surroundings. You will find many people playing with their smartphones and others who wear more gadgets than clothes. We are referring to those who use more than one smart phone, Bluetooth devices, wearable fitness trackers, iPods and so on.

Similarly, if you are in a position to determine the affordability and possesses the authority to make decisions, then we are talking to the right person.

People who do not qualify on these three aspects cannot make the decision independently. We can still speak to them because they may be the opinion makers but the person with AAA rating is the ultimate.

- What are their knowledge levels on the subject we are going to present? – For AAA Rated Person
- What are their knowledge levels on the subject we are going to present? – Troublemaker
- What are the top five things that they expect from us?
- What are the top five things they like?
- What are the top five things they dislike, are uncomfortable or anxious about?
- What are the top five questions we need to ask them before the presentation?
- What are the top five questions we need to ask them during the presentation?

- What are the top five questions we need to ask them after the presentation?
- What are the top five assumptions we need to list out before or during the presentation?
- What are the top five topics we want to discuss?
- What are the top five takeaways of the presentation?
- What are the questions we need to ask them? Remember, you will earn more respect and you will instil more confidence by asking the right questions than answering them well.
- What do we expect from them at the end of the journey? For example, do we want them to write a cheque immediately or should they just applaud and leave.
- Which are the authentic sources of information we referred to for the presentation?
- Who has this information within the organisation and what are their stakes in this project?

At this stage, you might be wondering. "Is it necessary to go through so much of pain?"

The answer is yes. Although this looks like a long list, it takes less than an hour to draw it up and in turn it will save you and others many productive hours.

Interest

Will a client give you business because they want to make your balance sheet look better?

____

> The two words, 'information' and 'communication' are often used interchangeably, but they signify different things. Information is giving out; communication is getting through.
>
> - Sydney J. Harris

Similarly, will your boss listen to you just because he is committed to doubling your salary this year?

No. People listen when it is relevant or is of interest to them. Everyone wants to find the answer to their original question: What is in it for me? Nothing else matters.

Measurability

It is either measurable or miserable.

As the famous quote, "In God we trust, others need to bring the data." implies it is important to present relevant data in each slide. Facts and figures in the presentation enrich the quality of presentation to a great extent.

Always remember two things while presenting the data:

- Present the right data
- Present the data right

If it is abstract, it is misleading. Drop it. Misleading information include the following:

- Any statement or a claim that cannot be verified
- Inconsistent and contradictory data points
- Incorrect data or false statements that challenge publicly available data
- Any piece of information that dilutes the main focus or distracts the audience from the prime mover item

Drop any information that is misleading

- Any information or claim that is not quantified will not qualify.
- If the information is verifiable, it becomes reliable.
- When the information becomes insight, it becomes digestible and memorable.

From Information to Insight. Ask the following questions before presenting insights:

- How relevant is the information?
- Will it be of interest to the audience?
- Can we interpret the information properly?

If we have a piece of information that is of reasonable importance and if we can interpret it properly, it becomes a useful insight.

. . .

Practicality

We need to make sure that the statements we make and the ideas we propose are practical. They need to be palatable and realistic.

Loudness

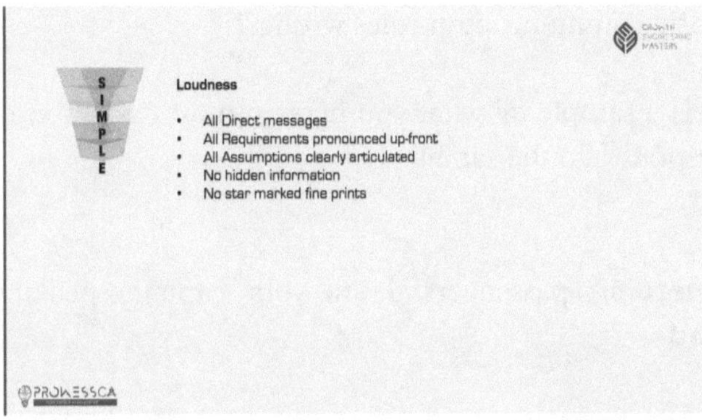

Points should be direct and convey the meaning loud and clear. Indirect or ambiguous messages will confuse, distract, and bore the listeners.

State the benefits, possible issues, and expectations upfront without beating around the bush. Everyone appreciates a candid approach.

> "Words - so innocent and powerless as they are, as standing in a dictionary, how potent for good and evil they become in the hands of one who knows how to combine them."
>
> Nathaniel Hawthorne

Direct messages send the right signals. Indirect messages weaken the signal and increase the noise. You need to maintain an optimal signal strength to noise ratio to tune the audience.

If you are a frequent flyer, you would have heard the flight announcements several times. Every time I listen to the muffled voice of a pilot through the public address system, it leaves me fuming. "How can even the smartest and most sophisticated pilots get the basic communication rules wrong?"

. Here is a sample of what you hear in most cases and our involuntary responses to the same:

"Good morning, passengers. I am your captain speaking. ….. " **Ok, Good**

"We are currently cruising at an altitude of 33,000 feet…" **What does it mean? Are we in the right direction? Are you in touch with ATC?**

"We are maintaining an airspeed of 400 nautical miles…" **Where is the conversion calculator? How fast or slow are we going? Are we on time?**

"The outside air temperature is -5 degrees Celsius." **What about temperature inside the aircraft?**

. . .

"We are facing mild turbulence. Return to your seats, sit back, relax and enjoy the experience." **Will we be landing eventually? If so, when? Until then, could you please switch to English?**

Ease

The presenter and the audience are at the core here. They should be at ease with the slides. The presenter should be quickly able to explain to them effectively and the audience should not find it challenging to understand.

Ease of understanding can be enhanced or compromised by the following:

- Text
- Text size
- Numbers
- Charts
- Colours
- Fonts
- Layout and formatting

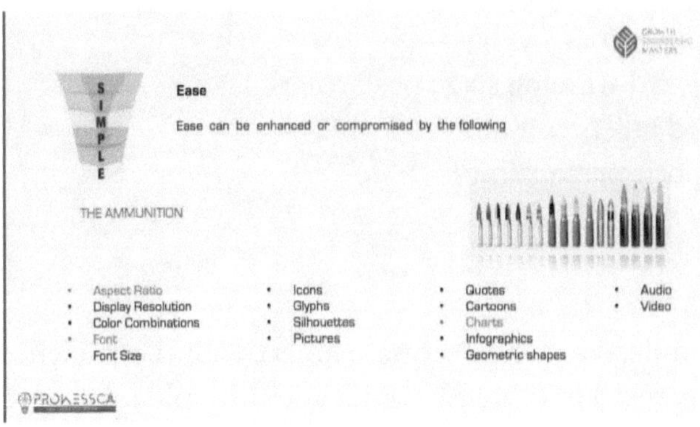

Look at the visual acuity diagram below. If you are not able to read the lettering in row 7, don't pick a text size that is smaller than the one in row 5.

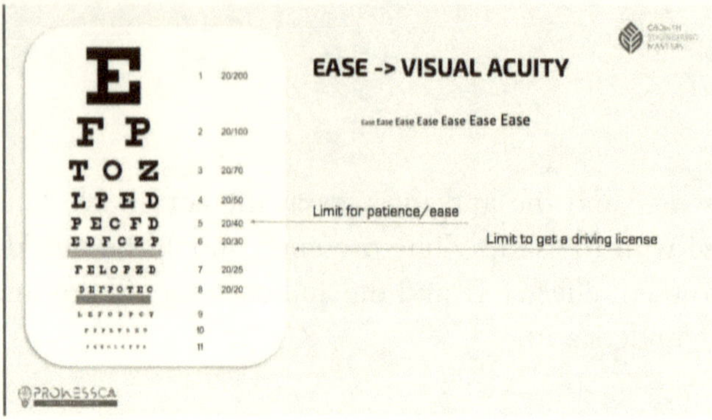

When the audience need an eye test or patience test, they will visit appropriate places. We don't need to test them. We also don't need to give them a treasure hunt experience.

What is common among the following classes of successful people?

- Politicians and statesmen
- Renowned lawyers
- Film actors
- Award-winning stage performers
- Ted talk presenters
- Sports personalities

They all understand the need to connect with the audience to drive their message. They spend significant time planning, preempting, preparing and practicing for their performances. For a twenty-minute Ted talk, some presenters rehearse for nearly 200 hours. As stated by Benjamin Franklin, "By failing to prepare, you are preparing to fail." So preparation is the key. Many novice presenters get into a situation called 'selective mutism.' It is a condition where the person becomes temporarily disabled or muted.

This can be avoided by following a structured preparation method. There are also many courses on presentation and public speaking skills. Books, workshops and training sessions prescribe several remedies starting from simple body language tips to complex yoga postures. While my objective is not to undermine those techniques, I can tell you one thing with certainty:

If you follow the steps and procedures mentioned above, your passion will drive your performance. You can experience it yourself. There is no shortcut to preparation. The SIMPLE method gives you a structure and direction. Assuming that you have a remarkable product or solution to offer, a presentation developed and delivered using this approach will increase the probability of your success by several notches.

However, we need to complement the effort put in so far with other things. Unless you are at a swearing-in ceremony, you cannot read out what's written on the paper or projection screen. You need to write a script that complements what's being projected on the screen.

You need to help the audience visualise the solution by walking them through a lane that illustrates their pain and gain.

Once they estimate their losses and gains, they will look at you as a credible person and consult you for a solution.

. . .

Body language

While you may have developed a stunning presentation, you will still need to deliver the same in a confident and credible manner. The audience tends to pick up cues from your gestures which in turn can lead to the misinterpretation of your message or content of the slide.

Mainly, you need to be confident about your body language before others try to interpret it differently.

It would be best if you adopt gestures that improve your credibility and enhance others' confidence in you.

While many books and courses do offer sound advice in this area, practice the following always for better results:

Today's technology allows us to rehearse and get instant feedback. Your smartphone becomes your best friend.

Download the app called **Prompster** Pro or something equivalent, to record and playback your script. As the name suggests, this app prompts you while talking so that you don't need to look at the projection screen.

Adjust and modulate the tone to emphasise on the topics, establish good eye contact with relevant people to target the messages.

Most importantly, always present factual data and speak the truth. Speaking the truth and conveying what you believe in does not require special preparation.

Presentation delivery

. . .

Once you have created the presentation, you may need to send it to your peers and supervisors for a review. Sometimes, you may even want to send it directly to your clients and prospects. Converting the presentation to a PowerPoint Show and emailing it is the simplest option.

In some cases, you may even want to host it on a public platform. Making the presentation public is the most comfortable option if you are unconcerned about the privacy, security, and confidentiality of your content. However, there may be some special situations:

- You want the presentation to be sent only to a select audience and control further sharing.
- You want to track who has seen your presentation so that you can contact them soon after they have watched it.
- You want to analyse the utility of the presentation and invite feedback to improve it.
- The email option is unviable because of the large file size of the presentation.
- You have used rare fonts which are not available on the destination computer or other devices.
- You need to get the presentation mass-printed and don't want your printing service provider to mess with the formatting and layout.
- Your presentation will be viewed using multiple devices with different screen resolutions.

In the above scenarios, the standard mailing options do not work. Let's explore the other solutions then.

. . .

PowerPoint, Slides and Keynote are not the only presentation tools available. There are many exciting and innovative products worth looking at. VideoScribe uses whiteboard animation. Regard them as a complementary service provider. Although we have more than a dozen products in the category, I am covering two (not necessarily the top two.)

Canva

Canva is an all-in-one online design platform. You can design presentations, flyers, CD covers, posters, social media banners and even invitation cards. This is what Guy Kawasaki Says about Canva: "Macintosh democratised computers; Google democratised information, and eBay democratised commerce. In the same way, Canva democratises design."

VideoScribe.co

This is a novel attempt to engage users. Videoscribe.co uses blackboard and scribble effects to illustrate a point. All the viewer sees is a hand scribbling on a blackboard while the background audio explains the concept. This gives the presentation an impressive look and ensures viewer engagement. VideoScribe is simple enough to master in a short time. The website offers video tutorials helping you learn smoothly.

Similar Products

- www.Slidebean.com
- www.Prezi.com

Audience Interaction

To bring in interactivity and improve the participation of the audience, you can take up various activities, opinion polls and so on. One such product that you can use for the purpose is **https://www.polleverywhere.com** This is an add-on to PowerPoint menu. You can set up a questionnaire and provide options.

Prototyping

Prototypes and design mock-ups could bridge the gap between developers and users and can potentially save lots of time, money, and frustration. If you have an idea of how your business application or website should function, you should try these tools.

https://www.powermockup.com

https://keynotopia.com

Prototype Designs using PowerPoint.

Keynotopia

Keynotopia offers excellent templates and UI elements for rapid prototyping. You are off the block in thirty minutes. Try this out if you want to contribute to the application development process.

Keynotopia offers multiple PowerPoint presentations with UI elements relevant to each platform. For example, you will find a presentation for iPhone 6, another for Android, others for Windows and so on.

Powermockup

Unlike Keynotopia, this is a PowerPoint add-in that seamlessly integrates with the PowerPoint itself. You will be able to use the UI elements the way you use graphics from the picture library.

You could ask the participants to respond using their phones, tablets or laptops via SMS, Twitter or other such platforms. You will get real-time updates and choices on the screen instantly. This is an excellent way to engage the audience and enliven the atmosphere. E-learning tools that resemble or make use of PowerPoint

E-learning

If you have used PowerPoint for training or designing e-learning courses, you will appreciate the functionality of Adobe Captivate. This is an exciting tool that works with PowerPoint and other applications and makes the e-learning courses interactive.

A similar product in this segment is Articulate Storyline. https://www.articulate.com. Both the products offer free trial versions that you can use for a month. If you are in the e-learning field or wish to design training programmes, you should try these out.

This brings us to the end of the presentation skills section. If you want to know more about presentation crafting, RFP response, proposal making, report creation or copywriting skills, I recommend that you read my book 'Slide Spin,' available on Amazon Store.

Fostering OPEN communications

Now that we have examined how to get our points across using our presentation sense, we will cover the rest of the modes. Remember the signal blockers we covered in the previous chapter? We identified eleven evils. These are the real communication blockers

- Anger
- Greed
- Arrogance
- Desire
- Envy
- Obsession
- Ego
- Aversion
- Attractions
- Inhibition
- Ignorance

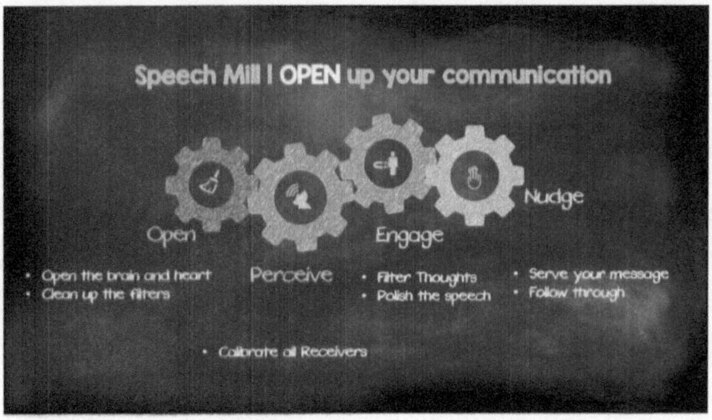

| OPEN up your Communication

Open

- Neutralise all communication blockers (eleven evils)
- Open your heart and brain

Perceive

- Understand the situation
- Focus on the topic and not the person
- Empathise with others in a similar situation
- Capture the reason and nature of the problem
- Ignore individuals or timeframes

Engage

- Create the urge
- Apply the SIMPLE filter
- Look through the prism

Nudge

- Get your point across
- Follow up for resolution

WORKPLACE RELATIONSHIP MANAGEMENT

Identifying and segregating our supporters and opponents will help us position ourselves better. You will know which door leads where and how to accelerate your pace.

Setting the right expectations and communicating effectively will improve relations, eliminate friction and conflicts. When you remove stress from your environment, you can be more productive and engaging.

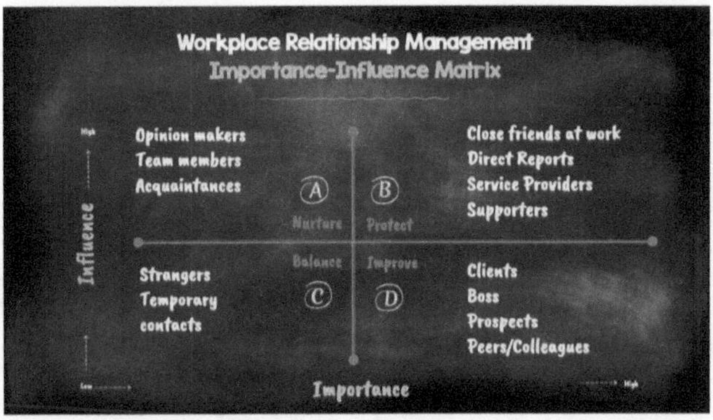

| Workplace Relationship Management

Look at the matrix. The 'X' axis indicates importance and the 'Y' axis influence. Divide them into four quadrants.

Category A – high influence – low importance
Category B – high influence – high importance
Category C – low influence – high importance
Category D – low influence – low importance

Arrange your contacts as per their importance and sort them based on how you can influence them. I have placed a few people in each category to illustrate the concept better. However, your quadrants could look completely different. You can download this worksheet template from gem.prowessca.com

Let's explore the sample quadrants:

. . .

Your direct reports, service providers, close friends at work, and other supporters come under **Category B.** That means you can influence them, and they are also of high importance to you. This team is the reason you are coming to work. This team gets you the power, promotion, package and so on. You will always need to protect them.

Your supervisor, clients, prospects, and other lateral colleagues come under **Category C**. They are crucial to your growth, but you may not be able to influence them every time adequately. Therefore, nurture these relationships. Try to visualise what quadrant they may have placed you in.

Category A members are the ones over whom you may exercise high influence but who may not be critical to you now. Try to guess if they might move to very strategic positions, and if you may end up needing their help. Place them accordingly

Category D people are distant souls. See if you need them and maintain a reasonably good rapport with them. See if they might also move to very strategic positions, and if you would need their help. Place them accordingly.

In the next sections, we will explore how to establish working relationships with each of them. We will also see how to set the expectations, delegate tasks to your team members, and so on.

This course is not about project management or product management. There are many aspects that we may need to consider during the product or project life cycle management. They are outside the scope of our focus for now.

. . .

We are briefly touching upon the critical aspects of delivery, project and product management because communication plays a significant role in each of these activities. Our discussion about communication sense is incomplete without drawing proper lines around our daily deliverables. The tools and techniques I am going to explain are more from a relationship management perspective. You may want to evaluate their usefulness before adopting them for other purposes.

DELIVERY AND DELEGATION MANAGEMENT

To ensure reliable delivery of your KPIs, you need to place influential people in strategic positions and delegate the work based on the team strengths and project requirements.

Wrong delegation of work leads to work piling up, loss of productivity and reputation. Tying the wrong horse to the cart will upset the whole thing. You need to have a mechanism to differentiate your team members based on their merit and contribution and assign projects accordingly.

You need to do a bit of team and task profiling before placing your bets.

Remember the sense and skill difference we learned in the previous chapter? Divide your team members based on the their sense and skills. Your matrix should look like this.

. . .

Now you have four quadrants:

High skill – High sense
High skill – Low sense
Low skill – High sense
No skill – No sense

People in **Category A** (Low skill – High sense) are like holy cows. They may not be very skilled, but they will have all the worldly wisdom. Chances are that these members are older than the rest of the team members. They are loyal and compliant people. Nurture them and support them.

People in **Category B** (High skill – High sense) are your work-horses. They not only understand the perspective but can execute projects also well. If you spend ten minutes with them, you will achieve ten-hour worth of productivity translating to high return on investment. Consult them, make them part of strategic planning and entrust them with supervisory powers. They are people who could replace you and push you to the next level. The more you trust them and the more you gain theirs, the more you will be looked upon as a hero.

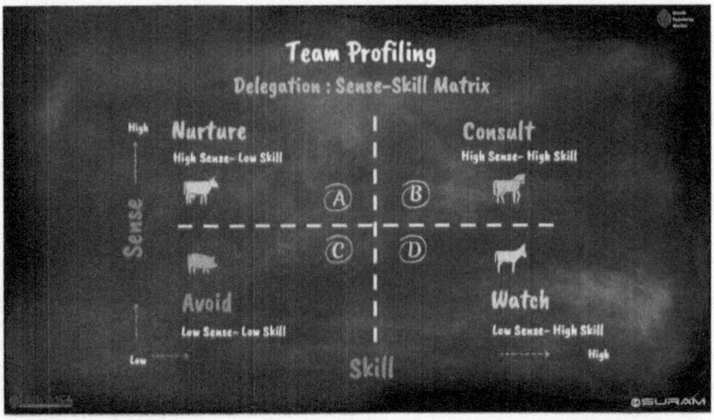

| Sense and Skill Matrix

People in **Category C** (High skill – Low sense) for want of a better expression are like donkeys. They are skilled but lack basic sense. They assume things and make mistakes. If they are conscientious, they will confess to their shortcomings. If not, you will need to detect the flaws and solve the puzzles in store for you. Chances are that these members are relatively younger than the rest of your team mates. You can pair them with those from **Category A** (High sense– Low skill.) They will have very complementary skill and sense combination. Optionally, you could get the Category B team to oversee them.

Over to **Category D**: Do not disturb them. Let their flow continue. Don't get in their way and take a hit.

You need to employ different methods to train, delegate work, clarify things and track them.

If you treat donkeys, pigs, and horses alike, the horses may run away, the pigs rest comfortably and the donkeys, turn on you. Unless you enjoy getting kicked by donkeys often, you should take concrete measures.

TEAM PROFILING | KNOWLEDGE - INVOLVEMENT

Those who work in assignments and roles where knowledge is more critical than skill the profiling exercise should be conducted differently. These roles could be in business analysis, customer service, public relations, and so on. Here, knowledge and willingness become critical.

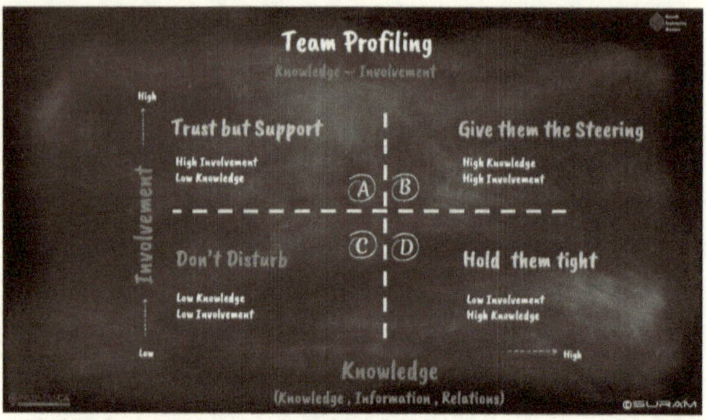

| Knowledge and Involvement Matrix

Again, take people in based on knowledge and involvement, and segregate. Your matrix should look like the above.

TEAM PROFILING | CONFIDENCE – CAPABILITY

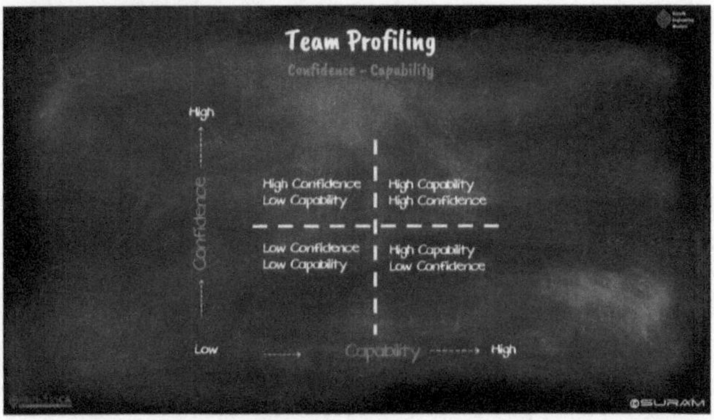

| Confidence and Capability Matrix

There may be situations where you cannot fully gauge the skills or knowledge levels of people. It could be because they are new, or you have no choice but to pull in more people to complete a project.

Then you can splice them based on their confidence and capability. People with low confidence will surrender and confess to their lack of ability. It's easy to filter out persons with low capability and confidence. For the rest, you need to assess their skills or include them based on their sensitivity levels. We have no issues with people who have high capability and confidence.

But the real funny characters are the people with high confidence and low capability. They are a menace who could bring the entire system down.

Fortunately, it is easy to spot them. Just ask them to rate their own skills. They are likely to be very generous to themselves. Ask them a couple of questions about the potential risks of the execution and how they will handle it. They will assure you that the project will never fail. Ask them whose help they proposed to take. They will be happy to drive everything on their own.

Ask a couple of more questions. Let other team members also assess. When you are assured of their low capabilities, just thank them and run far away from them.

CROSS TEAM PROFILING | COLLABORATION: INVOLVEMENT – INFLUENCE

Sometimes you need to rally people from outside your team to get work done. You might team up with another department or client team members. At that time, it will be essential to see who has the highest involvement and influence.

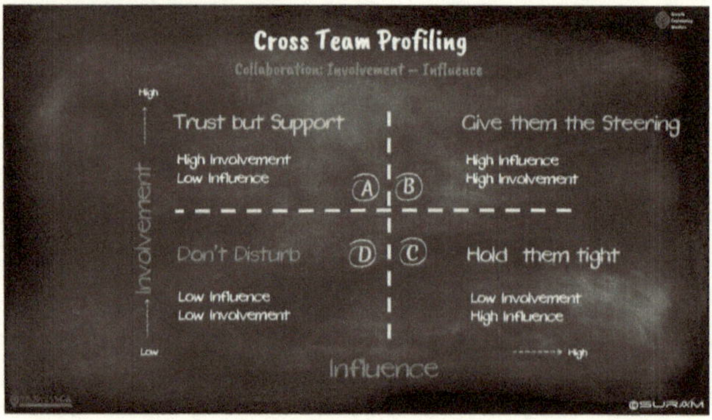

For instance, project sponsors are highly influential but may not have be involved everyday. Similarly, there may be power centres and prominent figures who wouldn't want to get their hands dirty. Your success depends on how well you can spot, segregate and pair them.

• • •

People who are highly involved but lack influence under Category A are trustworthy but expect support from you.

The diagonally opposite team who exhibit low involvement but high influence might trust you but may expect status updates from you. In case they are not your superiors or project sponsors, you need to lobby actively to get their support and pair them with those in Category A teams.

As usual, Category B teams are your best bets, and Category D should not be disturbed at all.

TASK PROFILING

After you have completed the team profiling, you will know who to include in which category. However, we should profile the task requirements as well before segregating people.

Many time management consultants will tell you that you will need to learn to say no. While it might save your time temporarily, it may have many side effects. Some of them are listed below for ready reference:

What might seem like an unimportant task to us may be life-changing for those requesting it. At times, due to lack of time or focus, we may develop a cognitive bias and wrongly attribute the reasons. This might result in a relationship rift. It could also become a critical task later

. . .

So just to avoid any subjectivity, we need to find a more logical way of prioritising the tasks. Even if we need to say no, we need to have a valid reason for rejecting it.

Even when no one is asking us to prioritise, task profiling is still an important activity to identify critical and strategic projects. You might be aware of or have used the Urgent-Important matrix for task prioritisation. I too did not know which task to prioritise and how. So, I created the following method.

TASK SENSITIVITY RATING

Whenever you need to start a new activity, project or task, ask yourself the following:

- Can the job can be delegated?
- Will it repeat?
- Is it coming from those in Category D?
- If not handled, will it become a crisis tomorrow?
- Is there a reward for prioritising the task?
- Will it be escalated?
- Will it impact contractual obligations?
- What is the task sensitivity rating score?
- Once you have the answers to these questions, get into deeper profiling.

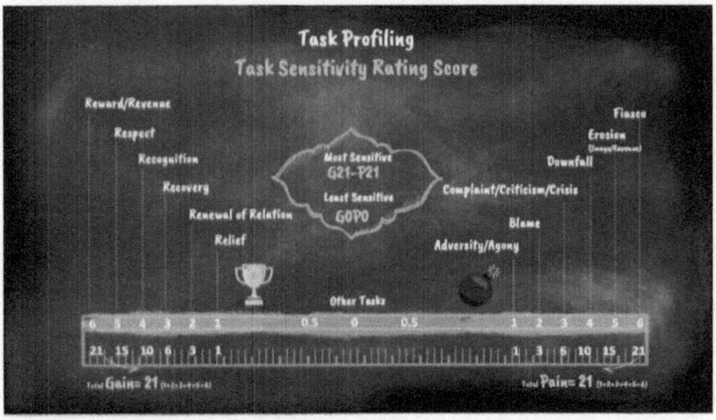

Task sensitivity rating

If you look at the scale above, you will notice two categories: The one on the right side is the gain and the left is the pain.

Executing a particular task on time , with accuracy, could result in three outcomes.

1. Significant gain
2. Reduction of significant pain or
3. Both.

We are assuming that the project is well executed without any negative side effects.

Doing a particular task could result in significant gains:

- Big relief
- Reconciliation after a spoiled relationship
- Recovery of a bad situation
- Huge recognition
- Respect
- Reward

Similarly, postponing or dropping a task without any forethought might invite one or more of the following pains:

- Adversity or Agony
- Blame
- Complaint, criticism or crisis
- Downfall
- Erosion of image or revenue
- Fiasco

The task can sometimes have more than one repercussion. For instance, doing a particular job can result in one or more gains and can relieve us of the pains also.

Let's suppose one of your old clients had an urgent requirement. He has been upset with you yet he approached you as a last resort. There is a regulatory requirement and therefore, if the task is not completed on time, the client might pass on the penalties to you, which may tarnish your image. If you complete this task on time, you can revive the relationship and eventually land a new project.

Let us find out the *Priority Score* of this project.

Pain: Compounded pains including loss of image and revenue: Item #5 (1+2+3+4+5) = 15

Gain: You are relieved, could revive a relationship, earn recognition, respect and potential additional revenue: Item #5 (1+2+3+4+5+6) = 21

. . .

Now total both the scores: Pain 15+ Gain 21 = 36

What is the maximum score we can have? Pain 21 + Gain 21 = 42

This task scores 36 out of 42. Therefore, this is a super important task.

The list of pains and gains are only illustrative. You can customise the list of pains and gains according to your need and assign ranking.

WHICH ARE YOUR NEEDLE MOVING TASKS (NEMOTS?)

Hope you have understood the importance of task sensitivity. The task sensitivity score gives us the tactical direction for your daily obligatory deliverables. Although very important, these activities are temporary and tactical in nature. We often tend to get busy with these activities and lose track of the big picture.

There are certain tasks which are called the 'needle moving' tasks. These tasks are more strategic and will take you closer to your purpose.

Most managers today cannot differentiate between an activity and result. Activity gets you busy. Result gets you reward.

For instance:

When you are closing a sale, sending the quote is a basic hygiene item. Following up with the customer is a regular activity. Giving him a discount or getting another customer to give an endorsement is a needle moving item. This activity gives you the final result. This is a needle moving task.

. . .

You may do a particular activity as a good-will gesture or as a favour. These tasks will not give immediate returns but may be of advantage in the longer run. This favour will enhance the relationship or your influence and will give you a chance to request for a return favour at a later date. This activity can also be classified as NeMoT.

Keeping an eye on your long-term or strategic goals is very essential for your sustained growth.

TASK PROFILING – PICK MATRIX

You can use the PICK matrix of Effort vs. Payoff by Bill Smith to find out the importance of any project.

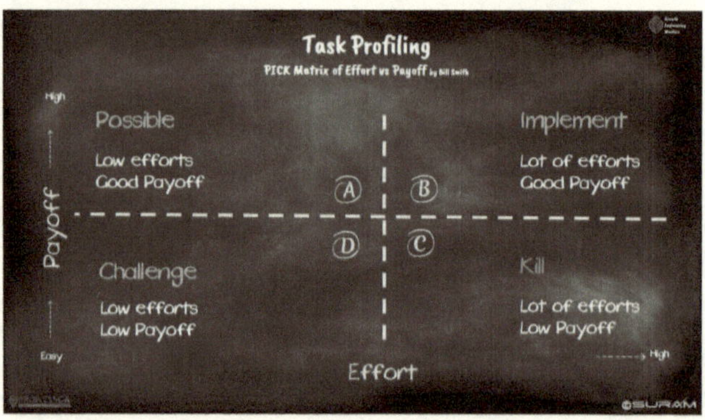

| Task profiling – PICK matrix

Create a 2x2 matrix of Effort and Payoff. Drop the items in the bottom quadrants. Pursue the top quadrants.

PROJECT MANAGEMENT TRIANGLE

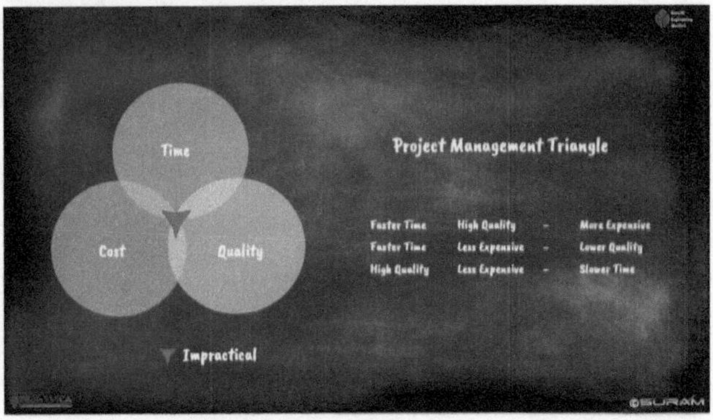

Project management triangle

Look at the diagram. Every manager is faced with similar challenges while dealing with clients. Clients want high quality, low-priced items in the fastest possible timeframes. We saw this phenomenon in Chapter 1. This is never going to change.

This is never going to change. As a manager, you need to strike the right balance between these three elements.

Look at the intersection. Though it is right at the centre, you may be cornered and secluded there. If you step into that small and red triangle, you might as well have entered the Bermuda triangle. I wish you good luck!

FOLLOW THIS PATH ™ FOR CLIENT DELIGHT

Having done the task profiling, team profiling, and project viability, how do you communicate them to the client?

| PATH ™ for client delight

How do you set the right expectations so that the client always stays delighted? Follow this path

- Deliver a bit more than **Promised**
    - Entertain no **Assumptions**
    - Deliver before **Time**
    - With a **Happy** face

CONFLICT RESOLUTION

During my college days, I used to have a strong desire to drive a car. One day, with a strong push from my friend and his instructions, I took the car out and drove it for a couple of kilometres.

The ride was bumpy but exciting for a while. Later, when I had to negotiate the traffic, anxiety took over my excitement. There were too many things to focus on. The grand adventure ended when I pressed the accelerator instead of the brake. It was such a disaster and an embarrassment. You can imagine the rest.

. . .

For over a month after the incident, I could not bring myself to think of the adventure. However, I reflected on the situation and thought about the key aspects of safe and confident driving. I figured that:

- We need to have a firm control over the clutch. It has to be extremely smooth while starting the car. If not, you will have a jerky start and it takes away half the confidence.
- We need to know the boundaries and maintain a safe distance.
- We need to be able to park the car in reverse gear and push it through narrow gaps between two vehicles. Obviously without touching any of them.
- We need the required skills and courage to climb over a steep road during a peak traffic.
- You need to have a sense of terrain and adjust your behavior accordingly.

If you don't master these five situations, the rest of your driving skills will not matter. The ride will always be bumpy. It will be full of anxiety, fear, and frustration. Sometimes it could even lead to road rage.

Had I not reflected on this and taken corrective steps, it could have become my weakness. The fear would have turned into a monster phobia.

But well, why are we discussing driving? Don't worry. I have not changed my profession. You are in the right class.

. . .

Like driving, communication also has similar key levers. Your ability to manage conflicts, negotiate and persuade people in various situations determines your mastery over communication sense.

If you manage these well, you will be able to navigate through any situation with ease. It improves your relationships and productivity. You will have a strong influence and many followers. You can almost eliminate stress and anxiety from your life.

Look at the developed countries. Despite so many advancements, most people convert a simple argument into a big fight and end up feeding the attorneys.

Some cities are full of underdeveloped humans. A simple disturbance on the road could turn into road rage.

But why do people do that? They cannot operate their clutch. So the first conversation is jerky. They don't have a sense of the terrain. They pick up fights at any place, anytime. They cannot drive through steep roads and navigate critical conversations. They cannot negotiate the situation or reverse their gears. You need to maintain the right balance.

It is particularly critical during the growing phases of the career. Too much involvement in conflicts may earn you the label of being a 'bad person.' If you don't express your feelings, you will suffer from resentment and frustration, and eventually implode. You need to reflect on this and take the corrective steps. Otherwise, it will become a significant weakness. The fear will transform into a monstrous phobia. You may be triggering many conflicts unknowingly. Your ability to sense and douse them will give you a lot of power. The world's most enormous fires could be extinguished with two mugs of water if detected at the right time.

. . .

Fortunately, there are ways. The pros have mastered conflict management. That's why they are pros. In this section, we will cover conflict management, negotiation, persuasion, and motivation. Let's suppose your mother-in-law gifted you a high-end sports car. You want to test its limits on an empty highway.

What will enable you to zoom your car faster?

Options

- Empty roads
- Wide and empty roads
- Wide smooth and empty roads
- Wide smooth and empty roads with no police checks
- The sports car on a wide flat and empty road with no police checks
- All of the above
- None of the above

Answer

None of the above. Sounds counter-intuitive but it's the brakes that help you accelerate. Without brakes, you will not muster the courage to cross even 20mph.

Conflict resolution is like a brake for communication skills. Without the ability to resolve the conflicts, you cannot advance in communication. You can continue to go ahead at top speed but you know what happens when the brakes are absent.

. . .

We will restrict our discussion to workplace conflicts only. We will avoid talking about domestic violence, sexual harassment, issues with the neighbour or fights in public places. You will still be able to apply these concepts in such scenarios. But I feel that conflicts at home should be viewed with different lenses. We should also avoid raising disputes with neighbours or in public places.

Question: When was the last time you jumped?

You are probably reminiscing all your acrobatic feats. This is because you assumed that my query was on physical fitness or adventure. No. That is a wrong assumption.

You just jumped to a conclusion. You may have jumped at your subordinate for something else. That is different. All assumptions are invalid unless proven. Let me repeat. All assumptions are invalid unless proven.

Unfortunately, we get into conflict resolution armed with a bunch of invalid assumptions each time. That is because we think we know. We only know lemon juice.

WORKPLACE CONDITIONS

It has been a long time since humans evolved. However, certain mental conditions push some people back to the pre-evolution phases. People with these conditions cause severe pain and stress to those around them. What are these conditions? How many of them do you have? Check it out.

Excusenza

These species are widespread. Whenever you approach them with any proposal or an initiative, they flash a crooked smile. They are consistent even during crises and emergencies. They corrupt people, spread rumours and while away most of the time. Where are they found? They are often seen freely roaming inside the cafeteria, lounges, unoccupied meeting rooms, or in front of elevators.

These guys are usually very early to meetings and tend to comment on the people who come prepared. Their slogan is, "Sorry, this is not my job."

This condition is as contagious as influenza.

Idontica

"I don't know anything!" That is the only sentence you will hear from them. These are *excusenzas* with a more severe condition. Whatever you ask them, they have the same expression. They retain all the qualities of *excusenzas* and exhibit some more stealth skills. They can embarrass the weak-hearted and sensitive people with their stunned expression of "Why are you asking me? Don't you know that I don't know anything?"

It is easier to bear a sciatica pain than tolerate these people.

Photophobia

These guys hate clarity, order and discipline. They breed and thrive on chaos, confusion, and turmoil. Try asking them to follow an SOP. You will be surprised to see how smart and creative they are. They will identify hundred flaws in the SOP and will tell you why it is substandard. For them, darkness is comfortable, and clarity is confusing.

Conflictophobia

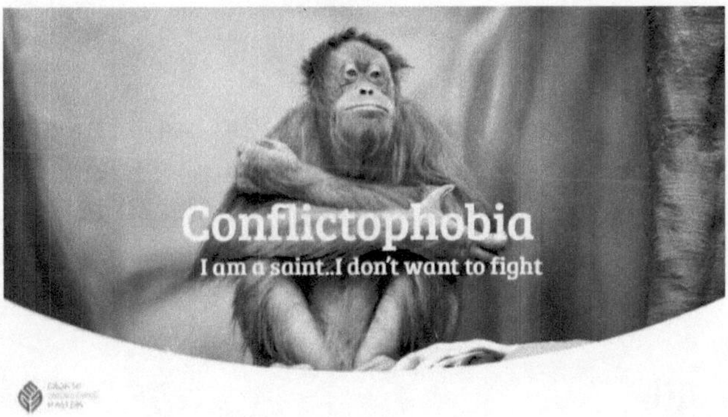

"I am a saint. I don't want to fight!" Such people don't want to argue, fight, or even frown. Come what may. Even when the deliverables suffer or someone ends up taking them on a ride, they have an undeterred will to just sulk and do nothing.

Blamerasis

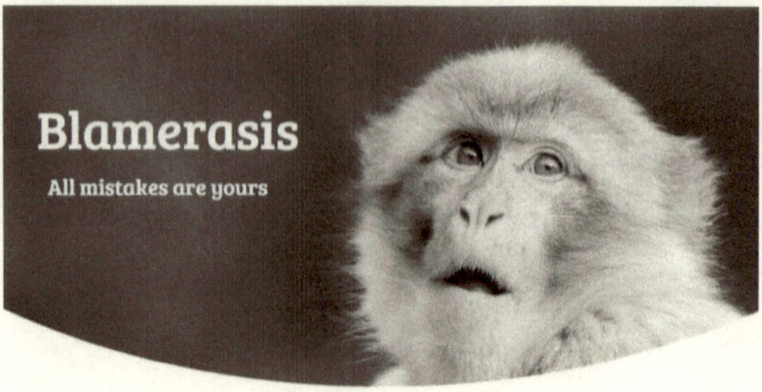

All mistakes are yours. Look at the face. Look at the expression. When you interact with such people, you will experience their unmatched creativity. They apply innovative methods to convince you that you have created most of the problems in the world.

Encephalitis

"I am brilliant!" They strongly believe that they are gods' gift to mankind. They feel their IQ levels are unbeatable. They are sorry

for others who work hard. Because they know everything, they can do things better than anyone.

Acrophobia

I am happy where I am. These guys don't want to take up any additional responsibility, have no career aspirations or professional desires. They practice minimalism in their career. They resent growth plans and criticise people with goals.

Glaikitia

"I will do everything on my own." The workplace matinee heroes. They are fully intoxicated by action movies and have a hero as their role model. A few words that you will never find in their dictionary: collaboration, team spirit, delegation of work or being sportive. Even when the deadline hits them or the whole world crumbles they hate asking for help.

Xerostomia

"I have a dry mouth." Everyone in the office craves for one thing: the opinion of the *xerostomians* on any initiative or issue. In the meetings, they only open their mouth to have coffee or water. That too, when no one is watching. They only nod or throw random expressions when someone asks their opinion.

Agoraphobia

"Touch me not. Leave me alone. Please!" They hate the limelight or focus on them; or anything that might drag them to the centre.

Myopia

"I cannot see beyond. Tell me what happened yesterday, how I can correct yesterday's mistakes today?"

They don't believe in tomorrow. Everything is here and now. They want to plan and visualise everything.

Chanjophobia

"I am afraid of change." Shock is the best expression. Period. They are allergic to change. You see the same reaction if you ask them to change their desk or even a pen.

Agitisis

"I know all the rules. But the rules do not know who I am. Rebellion is in my DNA." They are the active opposition leaders at the workplace. Nothing brightens up a room like their absence.

Menialepsy

"I am good for nothing."

Pissilepsy

"I am not satisfied with anything."

Binarosis

"Black or white only! No shades of grey, please. Tell me if it can be done or not. Tell me yes or no. I am not going to consider the efforts. I will not accept failures. 'No' is not an option."

Apatheosis

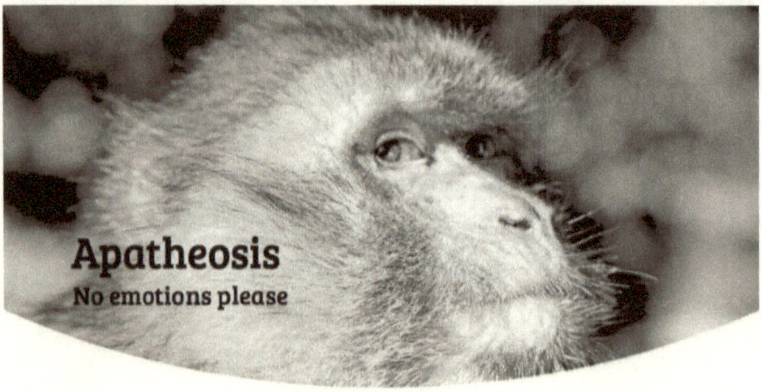

"Emotions? How do they taste? Sweet or salty? No feelings, please! Work is work. No emotions, only motions."

Favarosis

"Where is my boy? My team. My preferences. My favourites. My way or the highway. Please clear up."

There are many more characters. Those who have a comment or criticism for everything. Those who only say no. These who always escalate. Those who want praises each minute and so on. The objective here is to identify the common species, analyse the common ailments and causes.

But what is common among all these characters? If you watch them closely you will observe that they are stunningly similar and share the following attributes:

Aspirations : Low
Belief system : Faulty
Clarity : Nil
Discipline : Absent

Locus of control : External
Intellectual humility : Low / Arrogant

Motivation : Low and extrinsic
Goal Orientation : Nil

Expectations from others : High
Fear factor : High
Greed : High
Hatred : High

Openness : Low
Conscientiousness : Low
Extroversion : Low
Agreeableness : Low
Neuroticism : High

This is just a depiction of the most frequently encountered disorders. I chose the pictures of monkeys only to state that we seem to be taking a retrogressive step in evolution. I don't think monkeys harbour as many negative feelings, wicked intentions or cynical thoughts.

The idea is also to illustrate various dysfunctional mentalities. This should trigger a question: Do we need to pick an argument with such people? Are they not like other patients with mental health issues? We don't hate patients, but instead we extend our arms to help. Why are we behaving differently then?

Let us look at the pre-conflict scenarios to understand this better.

PRE-CONFLICT IDEATION

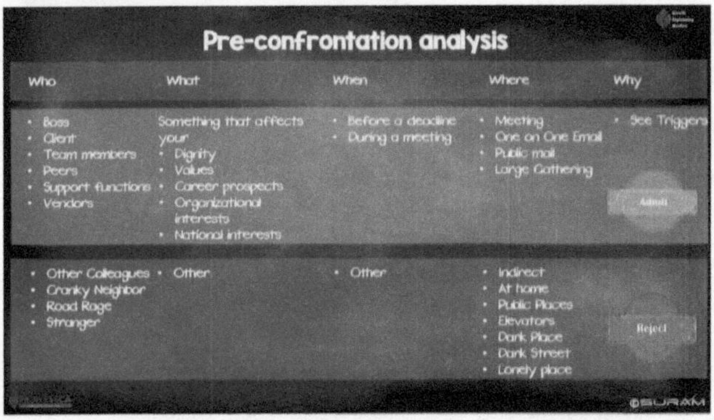

Who are we confronted with?

- Boss
- Client
- Team members
- Peers
- Support functions
- Vendors

For what?

Something that affects your

- Dignity
- Values
- Career prospects
- Organisational interests
- National interests
- When did this happen?
- Before a deadline
- During a meeting

Where?

- Meeting
- Over email
- Public mail
- Large gathering

Why did this happen?

Let's admit and analyse:

If a cranky neighbour or a stranger gets into a conflict in any of the following locations or instances, we just dismiss and move on:

- Indirect
- At home
- Public places
- Elevators
- Dark place
- Dark streets
- Lonely place
- Road Rage

In the last section, we have categorised our contacts based on their importance and influence. We have also agreed that Category B and D people are very critical for our growth and progress. As these relationships are interdependent we should not mess them up. We need to look twice before we move ahead.

. . .

Similarly, we need to be judicious with those in Category A and C. With all these people, if you make a mistake in your judgement, you will cause a permanent rift in your relationship. So proceed with caution. Let us now look at the actual conflict triggers.

Conflict triggers

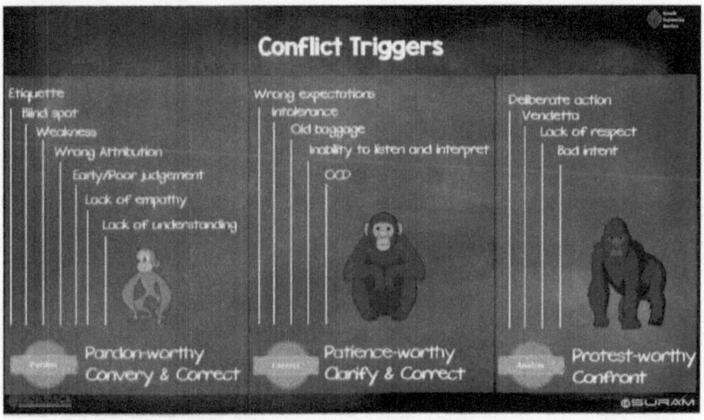

Three primary reasons can trigger conflicts.

- Blind spots
- Early or faulty judgement
- Deliberate and thoughtless action

Let us see how we need to react in such situations.

Pardon-worthy

. . .

If the conflict is likely to have been triggered due to any of the following reasons, we know who is at play here. We saw the play of evil forces in the last chapter. All such situations are pardon-worthy. We must give such people a couple of chances. We must, however, convey it and correct them too.

- Etiquette: Perhaps, they are not aware of the right behaviour
- Blind spot: It is their blind spot
- Weakness
- Wrong attribution
- Early or poor judgement
- Lack of empathy
- Lack of understanding

Sensitise people with etiquette issues and correct them slowly. Correcting a blind spot of someone is one of the noblest deeds that you can undertake. Early or poor judgement is a double-edged sword and causes the most damage.

Patience-worthy

If you think that the conflict was triggered due to any of the following reasons, this also should be conveyed and corrected. They deserve patience and consideration.

- Wrong expectations
- Intolerance
- Old baggage
- Inability to listen and interpret

- Any other obsessive-compulsive disorder

Physical or verbal abuse is not an effective communication tool.

With such people, you should try to :

- Set the right expectations
- Clear their baggage
- Use indirect instead of a direct method

Protest-worthy

The following acts are protest-worthy:

- Deliberate action
- Vendetta
- Lack of respect
- Bad intent

You should acknowledge and analyse this further. Don't start the attack. You should examine things thoroughly. You must gather support and escalate the issue if you are not the ultimate authority to punish them. Always demonstrate your standards.

When you want need to confront

. . .

First and foremost: Don't spoil any relationship beyond repair. Pride is about who is right, and humility is about what is right. Humility is always better.

Always remember that there is a police station inside your brain. Lodge your complaint first and let your opponent file the FIR. If it's a worthy case, we will proceed.

Your opponent will analyse the following:

- Does the situation warrant reaction?
- Does the situation warrant escalation?
- Can you handle it on your own?
- Is it worth fighting for?
- Is the impact temporary or permanent?
- What happens in the short-term?
- The mid-term consequences?
- Long term effects?

He will also consider:

- Were they triggered by you?
- Were they fuelled by you?
- Do you have any common shortcomings?
- Were there any other reasons?

Pros master conflict. That's why they are pros. Pros fight with their internal monkeys and win everyday.

. . .

There is an old Sanskrit saying, "You can make your friend drink poison, but you cannot make your foe taste even honey." You don't need to honour those monkeys as they never returned any favours. If the internal band of monkeys protest, just silence them and move on. Different strokes for different folks. Conflicts could become complicated in unequal relationships. Let me repeat: conflicts could become complicated in an unequal relationship. Open fights with your boss or client could prove expensive.

Each conflict is an excellent opportunity to create a stronger bond. Choose your tools wisely. Are you using an axe when a nail clipper is sufficient? Try following the 4T method to mitigate conflicts.

- **Transform:** You can transform the situation by persuading the other person.
- **Treat**: You can correct their mistakes and convert them into your loyalists.
- **Trash:** You can trash and dismiss the buzz and move on.
- **Tolerate**: In some cases, just tolerate it as much as you can.

When you need to confront your team members

At times, you need to correct the behaviour of your teammates. Vedic wisdom suggests the following method.

- Cajole
- Counsel
- Caution
- Crush

WHEN YOU NEED TO BE THE JUDGE FOR YOUR TEAM MEMBERS

Sometimes, you need to sit in the judge's seat or escape from being sandwiched. Follow the method below:

- **Separate** the persons, situation and the issue
- **Understand** the perspectives
- **Integrate** the parts and ideate
- **Take** everyone down the resolution path.

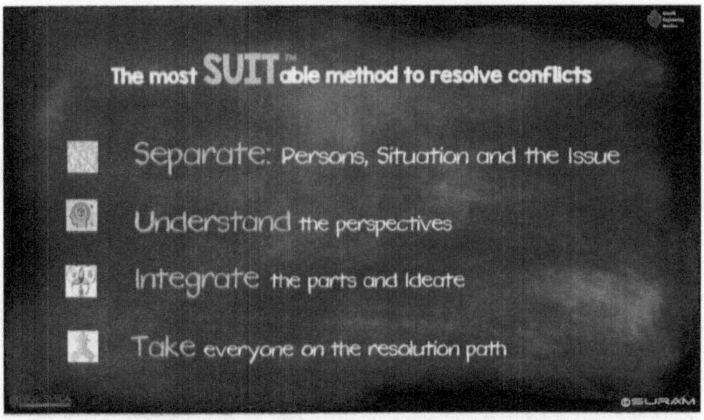

The most SUIT™ -able method to resolve conflicts is one that I have been using successfully for over a decade to resolve both internal and external ones.

Your prime responsibility is to resolve the conflicts amicably. Ideally, you should sense them proactively and nip them in the bud. If you don't resolve the disputes with your team members, performance and harmony will take a severe beating, and it will demoralise them . The leader needs to make team members accountable and show them the right path.

Here is an old lesson I learned during one of the training programmes. When you take the following steps, it is difficult for people to pick fights with you. Learn to say:

- Sorry
- Thank you
- Excuse me
- Please

These are the best STEPs you can take.

SENSING THE PAINS

Getting people to follow you without formal power or authority is called real leadership. Real leadership lasts forever. Your reputation, and the respect people have for you will undoubtedly outlive you.

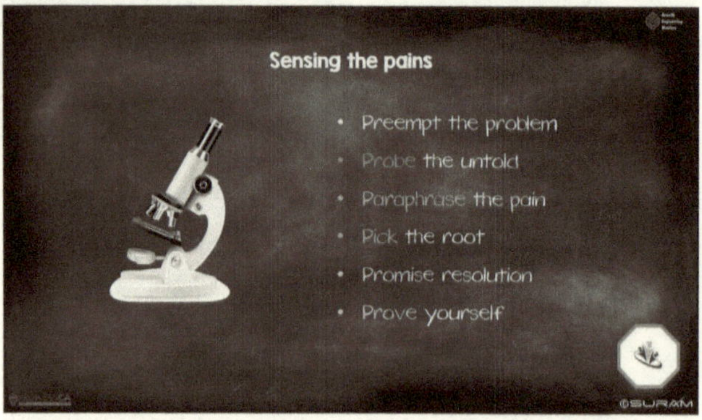

One of the most powerful and effective ways of nurturing a relationship is by continually sensing the emotional imbalance of your dependents and acting on it quickly. Your dependents are your family, your boss, direct reports, and the clients whom you serve for a living.

You always need to be vigilant of the emotions displayed by them. There are many unexpressed feelings. Not everyone is vocal. Not everyone complains. These are people who value relationships more than hassle-free experiences. You must certainly take care of them. You need to read between the lines and sense the pains. When you notice that someone is displaying a different set of emotions, you need to follow these steps:

- **Pre-empt** the problem
- **Probe** the unexpressed

- **Paraphrase** the pain point
- **Pick** the root
- **Promise** resolution
- **Prove** yourself

Always look them in the eye. You will be able to read their thoughts better.

When you sense trouble, probe them gently by sharing your fears. When you exchange your emotions the opposite person will open up.

Study the problem and promise them a resolution. Preventive care is the most effective and most appreciated.

Sometimes, angry clients or frustrated team members need little more than the usual care. Heal them as follows:

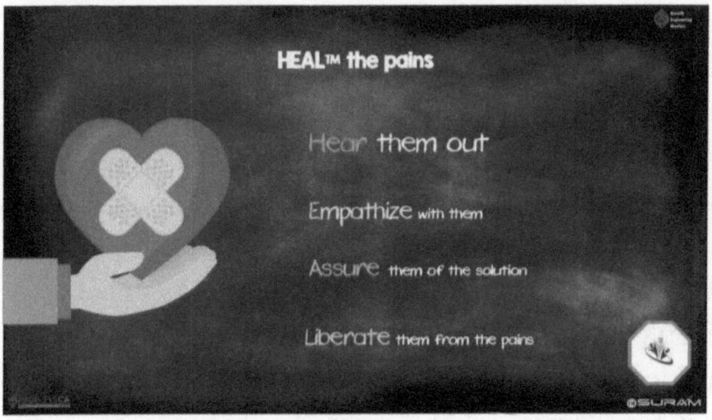

- **Hear** them out
- **Empathise** with them
- **Assure** them of the solution
- **Liberate** them from the pains

HEAL™ is an effective technique that I have been following for decades

Key considerations

- Let your sense of terrain prevail always
- Put relationships over ego
- Prefer war over a battle
- Choose magnanimity over pyrrhic victory
- Let your empathy bloom
- Let the IPS decide
- Use different strokes for different folks
- Conflicts can become complicated in unequal relationships
- It is best to avoid conflicts during the early stages of career
- Give importance to relationships
- Every conflict is an excellent opportunity to create a stronger bond
- If the internal gang of monkeys create a conflict, just silence them and move on
- Favours showered on monkey fellows are never returned
- Don't spoil something beyond repair
- Pride is concerned with who is right, and humility is concerned with what is right. Apply humility always
- Patience always pays

NEGOTIATIONS

You will often find the need to negotiate with people around you for many things. There are several excellent techniques for negotiation, depending on the situation. In this section, we will cover the absolute basics. I have provided several links on the portal. You could browse them and enhance your knowledge.

During negotiations, you must never assume that the slices of the pie are equal. It means that there is no reason to cut it into equal parts. In conflict scenarios, you need to analyse a few critical things. Is it necessary that you win all the time? Is it ok to okay to concede a point to get a better deal next time?

When two children are fighting for an orange, their parents walk in. The dad asks them why they are fighting. When both say that they want the orange, he picks it peels it, and makes two equal portions. The man was proud of his skills. He was able to use his corporate wisdom on his kids. But when he hands over the orange, he notices that both the children are not happy. That perplexes our corporate leader. Their mom steps in and hands over the peel to a girl and the orange to another. Our man sees the bright faces of both girls.

Why did this happen?

The first child wanted to eat the orange. The second child wanted to play with the peel. Corporate man thought he knew the entire world better than anyone else. So, do not assume that slicing the pie equally will solve the issue. The solution could lie elsewhere. When you cannot use equal slices of a pie, think of the next Best Alternative to Negotiable Agreement (BATNA)

. . .

BATNA was introduced by two Harvard professors *Roger Fisher and William Ury* in their best-selling book 'Getting to Yes: Negotiating Agreement Without Giving In.'

Let's assume that you approached your boss to seek a month's vacation. He wants you to get back to the office in two weeks. There is no way that you can return halfway through your trip. So, you agree half-heartedly to support him remotely through a couple of conference calls. That is your BATNA? What if you cannot comply? You need to cut your plans to half. That is called the Worst Alternative to Negotiated Agreement (WATNA.) Which one should you propose first? You should start by saying that you need 30 days off and could support remotely if need be. Never drag it till the WATNA stage.

Remember the old camel story? One old man had 17 camels. Before he passed away, he wrote the following in his will:

- Give half of the camels to my first son.
- Give one-third to my second son.
- Give one-ninth to my third son.

When the three sons wanted their share, they realised that there was no way to split 17 camels the way their father wanted.

So they approached an old man who added one more camel to the herd and divided them as follows.

- First son: half of camels (18 /2) = 9
- Second son: one-third of the camels (18 /3) = 6
- Third son: one-ninth of camels (18 /9) = 2

He takes away the camel he brought. Everyone got their rightful share of camels. So sometimes the solution can come from outside also. Remember to use your creativity and innovation to win in negotiations.

In negotiations

- An equal share is not a win-win
- Losing the argument is not a win or loss
- Losing a relationship is undoubtedly a loss

Negotiations following the approach below will be most fruitful:

- Do adequate research and find out what is in it for them.
- Be ready with all the points that demonstrate the benefits of your approach and the dangers of not accepting them.
- Come prepared with two or more alternatives.
- Connect with them emotionally and find common ground.
- Silence the monkeys.
- Clear all assumptions.
- Don't go with a win or die mindset. The win-win approach always wins.
- Be ready to walk out. Success loves brave people.
- Be prepared to give-in. It is not the end of the world.
- Don't convert the negotiation to severe conflict.

Persuasion

. . .

Sometimes you need to persuade people to take your path. It may be easy to convince known people and those you have a relationship with or can influence.

At times, you may need to persuade someone who may not know you fully. Use the following approach during such scenarios:

Robert B. Cialdini introduced these laws in his book titled '7 Laws of Unconscious Persuasion.'

- The Law of Contrast
- The Law of Reciprocation
- The Law of Commitment and Consistency
- The Law of Social Proof
- The Law of Likeability
- The Law of Authority
- The Law of Scarcity/Urgency

You must have noticed that many marketers and advertisers use these techniques on us. It is ok as long as you are pushing a genuine product and an ethical cause.

Engaging your team members

Nothing in the world is more promising and effective for your career than high employee engagement. The ingredients for stardom are the rest of the team. Period.

. . .

Your employees see your character more frequently and intensely than you see your face. Yes, just the way you read your boss like a book. Your reputation, your temperament, your commitment towards the job and their growth are noticed. Employees tolerate incompetent bosses but never a crooked one. Employees leave bosses and not companies. So, you need to win the trust of your team with your character strengths. Employee engagement has the following benefits:

- Higher efficiency and effectiveness of team
- Better customer experience for your customers
- Increased profits
- Your progress
- Your growth

To measure employee engagement, Gallup has designed a simple yet super-effective survey that constitutes the following:

- I know what is expected of me at work
- I have the materials and equipment I need to do my work right
- At work, I have the opportunity to do what I do best every day
- In the last 7 days, I have received recognition or praise for doing good work
- My supervisor, or someone at work, seems to care about me as a person
- There is someone at work who encourages my development
- At work, my opinion seems to count
- The mission or purpose of my company makes me feel

my job is important

- My associates or fellow employees are committed to doing quality work
- I have a best friend at work
- In the last 6 months, someone at work has talked to me about my progress
- This last year, I have had opportunities at work to learn and grow

It is called the Q12 questionnaire as it contains 12 questions. These questions dissect the engagement levels and give you an accurate picture. It is the sole responsibility of the leader to provide all requirements of team members stated above.

Make sure you run this survey once in a quarter and compare the results. You will be happy that you did it. It is not just a survey. It is a sure way. Take this lesser-travelled road to higher employee engagement:

- Set performance expectations: Give a clear understanding of KPI and agree on it
- Encourage autonomy: Don't nit-pick
- Trust and empower them
- Discuss growth opportunities frequently
- Encourage early failures: Failure-friendliness takes you closer to success
- Tell them the meaning and purpose of the job
- Offer a sense of protection: Support during crisis times. Keep sensing their pains and HEAL™ them
- Mix people with extrinsic and intrinsic goals: Do personality profiling and discuss their career goals and tell them how you can support them

The challenge-ability ratio defined by Mihaly Csikszentmihaly finds a sweet spot between optimal performance and engagement.

Maintain this ratio to keep the engagement high.

How to disengage employees?

Want to know how to actively disengage your team members and get mass resignations in your inbox? You can follow these time-tested methods:

- Triggering FUD fatigue
- Public bashing
- Wrong debits
- No recognition
- No sense of growth
- Signs of favouritism
- No differentiation of talent and results
- Exposing them in front of your supervisor or client

You see, it's easy. I promise. It works too!

SUMMARY

- The Open method of communication offers us a structured route to effective communication
- It is essential to profile our stakeholders based on their importance and influence to nurture relationships

- Successful delegation and empowerment fosters team motivation and engagement
- Prioritising the projects is easy when we use task priority scoring
- It is essential to set the right expectations with the clients based on time, quality and cost balancers
- We can follow a stable PATH to achieve client delight
- If content is the king, context is the kingmaker
- Design is the critical ingredient of a a successful presentation
- If we don't follow a SIMPLE method for presentation, we are complicating everything
- It is not necessary to have an equal piece of pie during negotiations. Win-win propositions and relationship fostering is the key
- Not all conflicts are worth a fight. Conflict breeding is not part of our growth plan
- During conflict resolution, it is essential to silence the evils and empathise with the other party
- Our reputation and reliability are determined by our ability to sense and HEAL the pains
- Ingredients of stardom are the rest of the teammates
- Q12 survey gives us critical lenses to achieve high employee engagement
- We need to find the sweet spot between the challenges and abilities of team members to draw the best out of them

5

DIGITAL QUOTIENT

"Technology is anything invented after you were born, everything else is just stuff."
Alan Kay

LEARNING OBJECTIVES

By the end of this chapter, you should be able to :

- Understand various technology trends that are shaping the future
- Appreciate the need to develop the digital quotient for three dimensions: career, workplace, and family
- Learn the key accountabilities at workplace
- Study the threat landscape and the impending InfoSec threats
- Understand how to protect yourself and your dependents from these threats
- Explore various efficiency drivers, tools and platforms

- Appreciate the legal provisions and compulsions surrounding the digital asset management

CHANGING TIMES

Tablet, tweet, WhatsApp, Telegram, spam and writing on the wall! A decade ago, none of these words would have made any sense or have held a completely different meaning.

Look at these brands. A decade ago, we may not have seen a majority of them. We may not even have imagined them. Now, they are part of our essential list. Some of them have become our vulnerabilities also. We cannot spend a day without touching at least one of them.

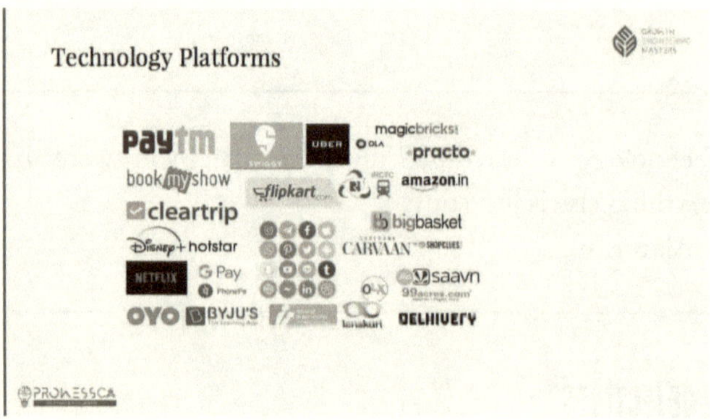

There may be many more than I listed here, but the fact is that the world around us has changed so rapidly. Of course, the digital transformer of the century award goes to COVID-19. Thanks to the virus impact, most of the technology changes will either be accelerated or killed. For instance, BYOD will take on a new meaning: bring your own disease. Some businesses associated with travel might have to alter their courses or completely wind up.

Similarly, we have many more surprises coming our way in the next five years. They will occur rapidly. We will unfold some of them here.

. . .

Quiz*

1. Who sells the highest number of cameras?
2. Who runs the most prominent music business?
3. Who is the competitor to the #1 Airline company?
4. Which theatre plays the maximum movie shows?

Think about the suitable answers for a few seconds

Who sells the highest number of cameras?
Samsung and Apple

Who runs the most prominent music business?
Mobile service providers, Amazon and Apple

Who is the competitor to the #1 Airline company?
Tele / video conference solution providers

Which theatre plays the maximum movie shows?
OTT platforms like Prime video, Disney, and Netflix

What is common among all these innovations? Successful integration of technology and process.

(*Extracted from the article "**Have Breakfast... or...Be Breakfast**!" written by Mr. Y. L. R. Moorthi, way back in 2010!)

. . .

What is likely to change further?

Let us look at some of the trends and statistics. The following data tells us many stories. As per a report by internetworldstats.com, there are 4.6 billion internet users as of December 2019.

By 2023:

- Nearly two-thirds of the global population will have internet access.
- There will be 5.3 billion total internet users (66 percent of the worldwide population).
- Mobile user-base will reach 13.1 billion.

At present, the total world population is 7.8 billion. Assuming the community touches eight billion by 2023, over one billion people would be wedded to more than one phone. Therefore, mobile polygamy will also be on the rise.

Cisco predicts that we will see 152,000 Internet of thing (IoT) connections per second by 2025. That means all gadgets, cars, websites and apps will start talking to each other.

Who knows? Two phones in our hands could start competing to offer screen time.

Cisco also predicts that there will be a 12-fold increase in AR and VR traffic between 2017 and 2022. However, I feel that VR consumption will be higher due to contagion fears.

5G implementation will boost video consumption further:

- Studies also indicate that over 90 percent of users engage with the video platform.
- There is a significant rise in voice-based search and e-commerce.
- In India, 5G implementation took a backseat due to COVID. It is likely to be implemented in the next fiscal year. Even if this gets delayed, we are likely to get Wi Fi 6. Though mostly experienced in a closed circuits Wi Fi 6 will be reasonably powerful. After 5G is implemented, all external gadgets and circuits will also benefit.
- According to Cisco, 5G will bring a 10 fold reduction in latency and 100 fold improvement in network efficiency.
- 5G is expected to boost the video content consumption further.
- This will accelerate content creation and consumption trends.
- This means, words like call-drop, lousy signal and video buffering will become extinct from our dictionaries. The next generations will probably recall them the way we talk about a trunk call or a rotary phone today.
- The number of interconnected devices will grow.
- The number of devices connected to IP networks will be more than three times the global population by 2023.
- There will be 3.6 networked devices per capita by 2023. Each of them will be connected.

Today, we are connected and supported by a global cyber infrastructure. Are we connected with reality, most importantly, with the future?

We discussed this in the previous chapter. The gap presents an opportunity. A bigger gap offers an enormous opportunity. What is that enormous opportunity?

TECHNOLOGY TRENDS

Let's revisit the technology landscape from Chapter 1

Artificial Intelligence (AI)

The world is slowly realising the power and possibilities of AI. Machine learning (ML) and deep learning (DL) are becoming pervasive. DL enables us to replicate some of the human capabilities in machines so that humans can get upgraded to doing better jobs.

ML and DL have already brought massive efficiency increase to several professions. In the medical field, surgeons can carry out precision surgeries. Online stores are pushing personalised content based on AI-powered search engine recommendations. Facial recognition has reached the next level since many organisations are using facial recognition apps to profile individuals.

Police can analyse user-behaviour and prevent crimes through the same methods. AI has already disrupted a few professions and is expected to disrupt many more in the near future.

> "One machine can do the work of fifty ordinary men. No machine can do the work of one extraordinary man."
> – Elbert Hubbard

Robotic Process Automation

Thanks to the pandemic, Robotic Process Automation has now taken a prime seat. Using AI-powered Robotic Process Automation bots, we can replace over 60 percent of mundane and routine tasks. This works exceedingly well because the bots are self-learning; they don't ask for a raise; don't display emotions or experience human wear and tear. This is likely to change the real estate trends as well. Since employees need not attend offices physically, office spaces will shrink and data centres will grow.

The great news is that, like other technologies, AI, ML, and DL engines are getting democratised, and the algorithms are becoming simpler to use.

To perform essential functions using AI, we do not need the help of data scientists and expert programmers.

Tools like Automation Anywhere and UI-Path are easy to use. We can use these tools to increase efficiency and scalability.

Natural Language Processing

. . .

We will have many more voice and natural language-based transactions powered by NLP. We can post queries, dictate, interact and transact using NLP.

AI-powered adaptive searches will soon replace the ever-complicated Interactive Voice Response (IVR) menus.

Low Code and No-Code Platforms

Software tools these days resemble beer. Youngsters are getting attracted to low alcohol or no alcohol beer variants. Similarly, we have a reasonable number of low code and no-code platforms for a variety of functions.

According to a survey done by a company called NetCraft, there are over 1.3 billion websites as of January 2020. Out of this, nearly 455 million websites are using WordPress, a no-code platform. Similar trends will emerge for mobile apps also very soon.

The most significant hidden trend is that over 70 percent of complexity is being hidden from the average geek. Several sophisticated technologies have been democratised and placed in the hands of power users with or without any coding experience.

We will review some of those during the latter part of this chapter.

Virtual Reality and Augmented reality

. . .

Virtual and augmented reality (let's call it xReality) is on the rise. There are already several early risers who created VR games, game zones and simulation modules to enhance educational and other experiences.

The fear of contagion could open up a demand for remote management with a more immersive experience. With the advancement of 5G and changed consumer behaviour due to COVID, more and more people will turn to video. This will trigger the use of interactive videos, virtual reality shows and augmented reality in daily corporate functions. There will be more virtual conference rooms, interactive training classes, sports and entertainment events. Let's take online shopping as an example. We have two variants in this.

Case study 1: Shopping in a physical store:

Using AI, AR and other reimagined user experience principles, we can walk into a physical store, browse all products on different shelves. Using the 360-degree view, we can feel the ambiance of the store. We can also touch the products by clicking on hotspots displayed next to the product to find all information about it. We can add the product to the shopping cart using voice commands. When you are shopping with your friends or family members, you can even engage with their holograms in the shop and interact with them.

We can even interact with real sales-people and get real-time demos. It would also be possible to interact with the other virtual visitors and acquaintances.

Case study 2: Shopping in a virtual store:

You can walk into a personalised virtual store of your choice. Based on your past purchases and shopping preferences, the virtual racks and shelves will be generated real-time with stocks of the latest products. You will be able to roam around in the shop, view product information, purchase products and interact with all your friends.

In both cases, network bandwidth will no longer be a bottleneck because of 5G implementation. Today, the latest tablets are capable of rendering complex 3D scenes very seamlessly.

Now the physical experience stores could be located next to the warehouse or in a deep interior suburb. The local guides can also walk you through the nearby places and sceneries and even send you the pictures.

Some products or popular spare parts can also be manufactured on the fly in the 3D printer store near your home.

Food delivery boys or Uber car drivers will deliver your purchases at your home along with your food within a few hours of placing the order. We cannot rule out the possibility of finding a self-driving bicycle also.

You will be able to do all these from your bedroom just by wearing an AR headset and probably a few data gloves.

Can we call this a 3D social shopping experience?

If you order emergency medicines, you may find that a drone has already delivered them at your terrace even before you could reach there. Who knows? We may need to install large post boxes on our terrace with biometric locks, cameras, and beacons that can coordinate with the delivery drones.

Business meetings: We want our conference calls to be more realistic and immersive. Our boss' hologram could flash at our work from home desk.

Travel and Tourism: It is safe to assume that most people don't want to physically visit any location for a holiday until the next year or so. There may be some travel. However, travel plans are most likely to be restricted to business purposes. Therefore, the tourism industry may come up with innovative ideas to provide an immersive tourist experience. So, we can soon expect to download apps that give us the virtual tour experience. Vloggers can become virtual tour guides as well.

Education: Students can walk into virtual campuses. A professor at Harvard University could be omnipresent at multiple college campuses.

Sports: VR-ready stadiums will give us a new experience close to watching our sports stars play live. The next IPL match could be played at a local YMCA playground, surrounded by green mats. Why? Social distancing. There is no need for fancy stadia that can host thousands of fans.

Wearable Consolidation: Since there will be a massive demand for AR headsets, they will be forced to become sleeker. So our next James bond gadget (that has the features of iPhone, Apple Watch, and iAR headset, and the like.) could be a fancy gadget that can perform all the jobs. This device should be able to switch the views seamlessly based on eyeball movements. This might rake up security and privacy concerns, but the world can regulate and adapt to it.

The proof is that today we are using many gadgets that James bond used in the films in the early 80s. Jokes apart, we need these as badly as ever.

We need to cut down on over 60 percent of the things we indulge in today such as unnecessary travel and overpopulation in certain places. Unsustainable and non-environmental-friendly solutions need to be avoided. If we can effect some real change, there will be a balance in the urban and semi-urban habitats; real estate demands will be uniform.

Technology may not be able to allay pandemic fears. Technology should be able make some of the things accessible to those who cannot afford it.

Many elders and incapacitated people crave for pilgrimages and experience of the sanctum. If a headset can fulfil their desires, a true technocrat could feel a sense of achievement. With very little, we have achieved enough over the last two decades to call the planet a global village.

Now, we can also call a village a globe too.

For a VR or AR experience to be immersive, multiple components are needed. Some of the critical requirements are

- Commercial availability of VR headsets at reasonable prices
- Availability of cameras which can record 360 degree views
- Ability to generate realistic voices on the fly
- Ability to generate complex 3D imagery
- Availability of useful Software Development Kits (SDK) and Application Programming Interfaces (API)
- Market places for graphic characters and animation
- A suitable device which can render all these
- Finally, a user who is interested in an immersive experience.

The last item in the above list is the key. Any product or service needs to have a compelling user demand. The epidemic has significantly changed the digital consumer behaviour.

If we don't discover the vaccine for COVID-19 soon, the fear of infection will change consumer behaviour permanently. Users will look for ways to continue with their lifestyles without compromising on the social distancing rules. Students will postpone their study plans abroad. Honeymoons will be spent on the terrace under the moonlight. Moms will refrain from sending their children to schools fully aware that school management cannot harp on alternate-day attendance. Therefore, point eight needs to be double ticked. We have made reasonable progress as far as the other points are concerned.

There is excellent support from Google and gaming companies like Nvidia to explore the possibilities further. There are over 50 popular Software Development Kits(SDK) and API interfaces. Amazon created a service called Amazon Polly that can render realistic speeches on the fly. Companies like Bose are using their sound technologies to enhance the VR experience.

Most of the tablets we use today can render complex 3D imagery. There are a good number of market places that supply realistic characters and programmes. Adobe is pioneering several initiatives on VR across animation, gaming, learning and so on. Using Adobe Animator, we can create interesting interactions while playing with the software. Similarly, Adobe Captivate, the e-learning and authoring tool has several features to support enhanced learning experience using AR and VR. Adobe XD generates rapid prototypes of VR experience designs.

The VOID (https://www.thevoid.com) is an immersive virtual reality destination. With several VR gadgets and wearables, they engage us with a hyper-reality experience. The opportunities are immense. We can take up time travel, enter a simulation, experience an 8D AV and do a lot more.

There are VR gaming zones that not only offer exciting games but also simulations. That means you can do a net practice of cricket or badminton that provide real-time analysis of your performance. This could be extended to all sports. Such training sessions will be beneficial in fields where micro-precision and timing are crucial. For example, frogs could be the happiest creatures as biology students need not dissect them physically to learn anatomy.

Similarly, a medical student or a surgeon now has endless possibilities in front of them. Add a DL capability to this experience. We will soon have AI coaches who can learn from real world coaches and unveil several new possibilities that were beyond human comprehension.

. . .

A portal called virtualspeech.com trains sales executives and next-generation leaders on presentation and public speaking skills with live feedback and analysis. What more can we ask for? A company named Vive (https://enterprise.vive.com/eu/dms), is doing pioneering research in this field and producing several VR paired devices. They already have several case studies that have effectively employed VR for practical purposes.

There are many more players and emerging leaders in this space, like Rumii and https://eonreality.com.

Internet of Things (IoT)

If you have used any of the following, you have already used IoT:

- A smartphone and a smartwatch
- Smart bulb
- Alexa

Today, we can integrate IoT solutions into simple devices that cost below USD 100.

For instance, you can control all appliances in your room (like lights, fans, AC and music systems) using a simple device. Does this mean machines will soon replace men? Not at all. Each of these advancements will make our life simpler and open up more jobs.

. . .

Trust me. During the 90s, when emails and mobile phones came into the market, several people went into panic mode. They complained about privatisation, and what not. Look at what has happened now.

VERTICALS WITH A VAST SCOPE TO USE TECHNOLOGY EFFICIENTLY

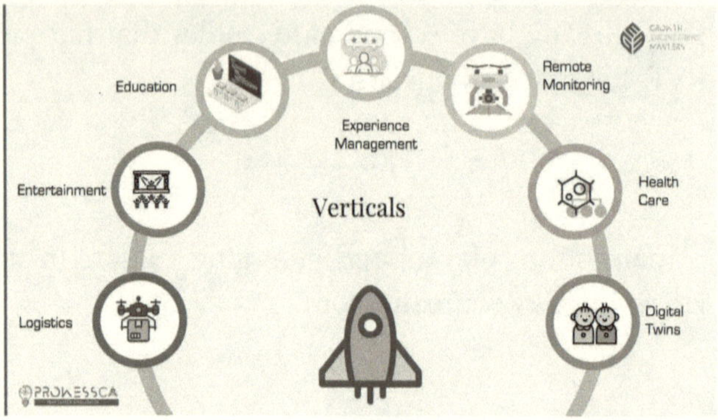

In the wake of COVID fears, the following verticals can make the best use of technology and disrupt their regular processes:

- Education
- Entertainment
- Logistics
- Remote monitoring
- Healthcare
- Digital twins
- Experience management

DIGITAL QUOTIENT

You need to acquire the digital quotient in three dimensions.

- Your career growth
- Workplace productivity
- Home computing

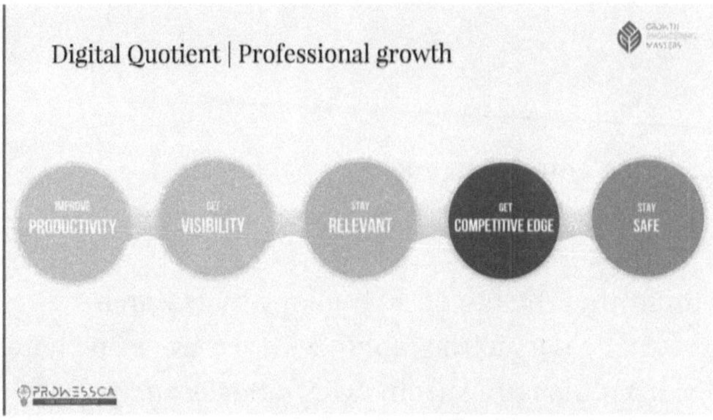

These are three separate tracks, and each of them have a significance of their own.

Digital technology for professional growth includes the following objectives:

- Improving productivity
- Getting visibility
- Staying relevant
- Getting a competitive edge
- Staying safe and secure

Digital at the workplace refers to productivity at your workplace and its utility in shaping your career growth. Some of the aspects include:

- Enhancing the efficiency and effectiveness of your team
- Advising and implementing the right technology (if you are a techie)
- Accomplishing 'augmented automation'

- Deploying the right tools to optimise resource utilisation
- Driving agility and scalability

Digital for home computing include:

- Monitoring the use of technology by children
- Assisting elders in the family with the use of technology
- Securing the family from cyber-attacks and privacy threats

Personal tech-savviness

There is a thin line between professional growth and career growth. Your day job may require you to do certain things in a specific manner. However, you can pursue your passions and grow your professional life and eventually align them.

Irrespective of the differences, you need to be tech-savvy to be able to lead. Please answer the following questions.

- Most of my files are stored on the cloud
- Over 95 percent of my savings and investment activities are on a mobile
- I perform over 80 percent of my tasks (utility payments and bookings and the like) using relevant apps
- I use a productivity tool for time and task tracking
- I have a secure personal network at home
- I use screencast tools and devices

- I have an e-learning portal subscription for my children
- I have a smartwatch to manage my physical fitness goals
- Most of the health devices I use are interconnected and blue tooth enabled
- My primary source of information before any purchase are online reviews and recommendation sites
- I have automated some of my routine tasks using applications like IFTT
- I think self-driving cars will be the next big thing
- I think robots can replace some of the jobs at my workplace in the next two years
- I use the voice assistant to accomplish basic jobs
- I believe AI can effectively solve some of the problems we face at the workplace
- I subscribe to technology newsletters and watch YouTube videos to stay updated on the latest technology
- I read magazines from apps like Magzter, Zinio, Issuu and the like
- My friends and colleagues call me when they face issues with IT applications or devices
- I understand what my children do using their laptop or desktop
- I keep myself updated on various cyber-crime issues and fix my vulnerabilities

These twenty items are hygiene factors. Assign one mark for each.

If you have scored less than ten chances are that you have a gap. You may be finding it difficult to cope with technological changes. You may not pitch ideas on automation or other product development. If this gap widens, you will not enjoy your work.

. . .

Please do write to me at sr@suram.me about your concerns with the subject line 'Tech Gap.' Although I cannot guarantee an immediate response, I will certainly try my best to assist you in overcoming your challenges.

If you have scored between ten and fifteen, you seem to be doing well. But like most other thing, what you don't know will always haunt you. Take up the assignments I suggested in this chapter and keep watching the videos. Technology is everything now. The epidemic has decided so. Please do not loosen your grip on it.

If you have scored more than sixteen – good going! You will still need to validate your knowledge against your contribution mentioned in the following questionnaire titled 'Workplace Digital Maturity.' Personal tech-savviness should reflect in the professional and career aspects too. Tech skills and service orientation go well together.

Digital at the workplace

The tech-savviness of your team and the key functionaries at work determine the future course of your organisation.

. . .

Answer the following questions. You may not be involved or accountable for any of these. However, this maturity will have significant impact across the organization and determines the future.

Work place digital maturity

- We have a mobile-optimised version of our web site
- Both website and mobile versions consistently respond under two seconds
- Customers can purchase our products and services online and offline
- They can view the real-time workflow and interact with us
- Customers can reach us through multiple channels to register their requests and complaints
- We track visitor conversions, visitor-drops and reach out to them
- All interaction channels offer a seamless handoff
- All our interactions are recorded, and quality reviewed
- Over 70 percent of work done is on core applications
- For the remaining activities, we have implemented Robotic Process Automation
- All support functions (like Recruitment, HR Operations, Application Development, Product development, Desktop support, Infrastructure support, Quality, Training, Procurement, Finance, Audit, Legal, Communication, InfoSec, Facilities management and Logistics) have mature digital applications
- Our training teams have the latest tools to track and fulfil the training needs
- We have a full-fledged analytics team with well-monitored KPIs
- We have a full-fledged digital initiatives team with well-monitored KPIs

- We have a single place central repository of truth recording for every event
- All our applications connect with the external world as applicable
- Most of the interactions are gamified
- We have a mechanism to track and reach silent customers
- We have a history of preventing client migrations
- We have a reasonably good conversion and repeat purchase rate
- Our online ratings across all review sites is more than 4.5 stars
- We have well-laid and well-tested processes for exception management
- All touchpoints reflect the latest information
- We have tested procedures for measuring employee and customer engagement.

Your workforce contains both humans and bots. These bots could be any one or all of the following:

- Core business platforms
- Productivity tools
- Other interconnected business apps
- RPA bots that connect each of them

Standalone siloed applications and worksheets with macros do not count. They are as dangerous as malware programs.

If you have not started employing RPA robots, please start soon. Over 90 percent of the employees can automate at least 25 percent of their work irrespective of their job function and organisation maturity. You need to identify your bots, and make both employees and bots accountable.

Apps are accountable for enhancing productivity, fostering employee engagement and collaboration.

Understand that the only way to ensure optimal productivity is through a combination of humans and bots. Therefore, master augmented automation. As a leader, you need to operate at the intersection and continuously watch the connections. Connect your workforce and facilitate the collaboration. RPA platforms like UI-Path have community versions and are relatively economical. Try out the trial versions. Low code and no-code platforms help you to stay productive. Consider using the following platforms (or their equivalents.) Your team members and yourself could reap rich productivity gains. You don't need to be a techie to use any of these:

- Design brochures, flyers, logos, presentations : Canva
- Develop and host websites: WIX
- Develop and host websites: Render forest
- Connect and automate/ api connector: IFTT , Zapier
- Transform the way you work & collaborate: AirTable, AppSheet, Caspio, and FileMaker
- Find talent and outsource: Fiverr, upwork, PeoplePerHour, Workana, Freelancer
- Latest tech bytes on YouTube: Savjee
- Develop mobile apps instantly: Famous
- Become a web guru without coding: WordPress
- Develop mobile apps without coding: AppyPie
- Browser with a difference: Biscuit
- Knowledge management and organisation tool: Notion

You should spend at least five minutes on each of the above tools in case you are serious about any one of the following:

- Increasing your productivity
- Getting additional income through freelancing
- Improving your relations and gross utility
- Understanding the general direction of this world

Productivity with Outlook

While some people are immersed in social media others live inside their inboxes. This is an indicator of the way we spend the time, our mood and even relationship status.

If you receive only least five or six emails in a day, you can manage your work well. But many managers in the corporate world, receive over 200 mails every day and have to act on at least a few of them the same day delegating and tracking the progress. I am not sure if success begets success every time, but mails beget numerous mail threads each time with near-zero productivity.

Here, I am giving you some productivity tips and time savers:

- Smart folders (sorted into Overdue, Due Today and Reminder)
- Dictation
- Rules
- Protocols using Mentions
- Add-ins for project management and collaboration
- Calendars

Smart folders:

The newer version of Outlook comes with smart folders. Setting up a smart folder is very simple. You just have to search inbox for any item and launch the advanced search. There you select labels such as due for today, overdue and reminder. Save each of them under respective names. Outlook creates smart folders automatically. You no longer need to search for actionable emails in the inbox or sent items. You will find all of them at the same place.

Similarly, some team members need extra push and daily reminders. You can segregate and chase them whenever you have time. Your star performers usually don't need reminders. They may need some help at times. So, you can create alerts just to enquire if everything is going well.

Dictation:

The new Outlook 365 for windows also comes with a dictation option. It is quite versatile and can compose sentences with very few or no mistakes. This feature is a big-time saver. For Mac users, this facility is available strangely in Word and PowerPoint. You can make use of it in the same way.

Rules:

Outlook rules need no introduction. You categorise and organise emails based on the from address and other parameters. If configured well, it can save a lot of time and strain.

Protocols using @Mentions

In the last chapter we discussed Denial of Service Attackers (DOSAs.) They inundate our inboxes with emails.

DOSAs and rebellious employees have a habit of sending emails to the entire world for every small occasion. They want to prove that they work hard. Such emails are great weapons for them to threaten colleagues and also gives them topics to discuss at the cafeteria.

You could tell your team members to use @mention tags to keep everyone in the loop so that the members know if the mail is FYI or FNA.

Once you set this discipline, you can create another smart folder with emails mentioning you. You can prioritise and act on them while reading others at leisure.

Add-ins for project management and collaboration

Add-ins extend the functionality of any standard application. In the case of the MS office, several smart developers offer solutions for missing features through add-in functions. While there are hundreds of such add-ins, you need to choose the ones that add to your productivity and collaboration. For instance, there are add-ins for popular project management applications like Asana, Trello and others. You can open a Trello card from a mail or create the Asana task, update it, and so on. There are no upper bounds for this.

There are many other ways of being productive using emails. However, consider the following:

. . .

Minimise mails wherever you can talk and sort out issues.

If you send multiple signals to your teammates with follow-up messages, some of the best team members might get frustrated and will soon start searching for a better boss and may even be successful in finding one. The rest of the team members will get used to the follow-up culture and will never move a thing without a reminder. There is an old saying, "You cannot train a horse by shouting and expect it to obey whispers."

Follow the etiquette and force your team members to respect the protocols.

Observe people who build cases using emails. Filter them out.

Use mails sparingly. Tools have to work for us and not vice-versa.

Calendars

Missing important personal and professional events could cause great embarrassment and regret. You can avoid such issues by updating multiple calendars and importing them from different sources. It is a good idea not to mix calendars because multiple items can clutter and overwhelm you. It will pose a problem when you want to share a calendars. Therefore, maintain at least two separate calendars.

Creating calendar entries is easy. When an email invitation arrives, you can drag the mail item to create a calendar event. Check your calendar at least twice: before you begin the day and at end the day.

. . .

DQ | Skills that pay

Look at the top skills that are trending in the freelance world. Freelancing is emerging as a dignified and lucrative alternative to full-time employment. In the pandemic- induced pre-recession phase, gig economy could furnish some answers:

Top skills and their average hourly rates

Bitcoin – $215
Image object recognition – $180
Virtual machine – $175
Google AdSense API – $150
Behavioural design – $195
Lead magnet – $150
Hotjar – $130
Citrix / GoToMeeting – $125
Video processing – $110
Pitch deck – $105

Source: Upwork

This data was sourced from the Upwork database and is based on average hourly rates charged by US freelancers from Jan 1, 2019 – June 30, 2019. Each skill came with a minimum of two contracts and 40 billed hour (the equivalent of one week of work and more than one project) for reliability.

DQ | PERSONAL AND FAMILY

In this information age, where every child has access to unlimited internet, parents must keep a tab on the child's browsing activity and behaviour. It is counterproductive if the parent controls the child's behaviour with a carrot and stick approach. Parents needs to have sufficient digital intelligence to understand that their children need to have adequate digital quotient.

DQ Institute has formulated three levels of maturity:

Level 1- Digital Citizenship: The ability to use digital technology and media in a safe, responsible and effective way.

Level 2- Digital Creativity: The ability to become a part of the digital ecosystem by co-creating new content and turning ideas into reality using digital tools.

Level 3- Digital Entrepreneurship: The ability to use digital media and technologies to solve global challenges or create new opportunities in the digital economy by driving entrepreneurship, jobs, growth and impact.

The DQ Institute has studied its impact on children's risky behaviour online. The image below presents a scary picture of the correlation between DQ and child safety.

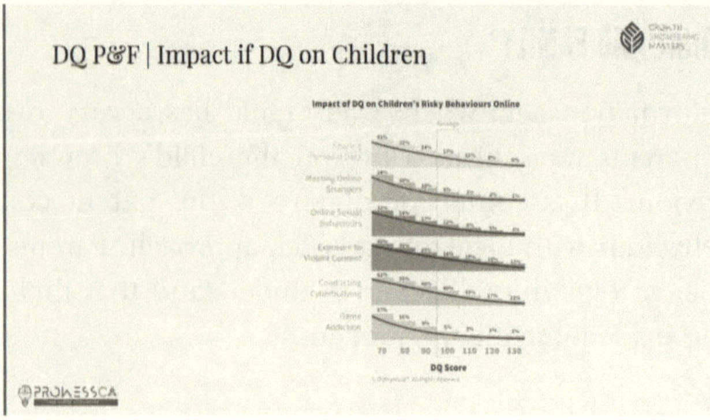

A child with DQ level of 70 has a 24 to 32 percent chance of meeting online strangers and learning online sexual behaviour. Fortunately, the likelihood drops to one to three percent for those with a DQ level of 130. This is a no-brainer. It is the responsibility of every parent to take all efforts to increase the DQ levels of their children and their peers.

The institute has formulated eight pillars that drive child behaviour and outcomes.

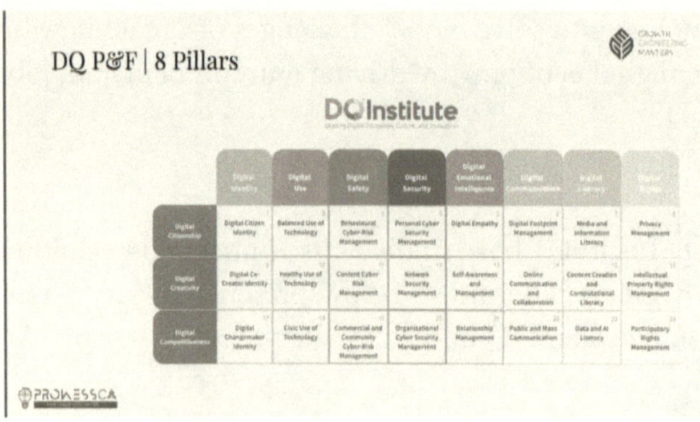

Digital Citizen Identity: Ability to build and manage a healthy congruent identity online and offline with integrity.

Screen Time Management: Ability to manage one's screen time, multitasking, engagement in online games and social media with self-control.

Cyber Bullying Management: Ability to detect cyber-bullying situations and handle them wisely.

Cyber Security Management: Ability to protect one's data by creating strong passwords to manage security threats

Privacy Management: Ability to be discreet in sharing personal information online to protect their privacy.

Critical Thinking: Ability to distinguish between true and false information, good and harmful content, and trustworthy and questionable contacts online.

Digital Footprints: Ability to understand the nature of digital footprints and their real-life consequences and to manage them responsibly.

Digital Empathy: Ability to be empathetic towards others' needs and feelings online.

Each of these pillars combined with the levels give you a list of 24 competencies. As a parent of twin children, I cannot think of a more effective and philanthropic model than this.

CYBER SECURITY AND INFORMATION SECURITY

With the advancements, there is also an acute need for containing and curbing cyber-crime. While the world was grappling with COVID over 40 million new malware samples were detected during January and April 2020. In 2019, over 144.91 million new malware samples were discovered.

Just to give a glimpse of the cyber-crime menace, let us compare the amount of money spent on IT projects and compare it to cyber-crime damages. The worldwide IT spending was estimated to be around $3.7 trillion in 2019. Cyber-crime damages cost the world $5 trillion at the same time. So, we are losing much more than what we are achieving. The worldwide spending on cybersecurity is forecasted to reach $133.7 billion in 2022. The dark web (that is not indexed or accessible through search engines) is estimated to grow 5,000 times larger than the surface web.

With more IoT devices getting connected, millions of devices are vulnerable to hacking. The worst impacted will be those wirelessly connected through digitally monitored and implantable medical devices. Similarly, today's smart cars also run a risk of being hijacked. Elsewhere in the world, people have already fallen prey to these sophisticated crimes including online murders. Yes, you read it right, online murders.

Make sure that you and your family members practice safe computing methods. Safe computing is your responsibility.

DQ | LEGAL FRAMEWORK

Most countries have elaborate laws on the following:

IT Privacy
- Personal Data Protection
- General Data Protection Regulation (GDPR)

Make sure you are aware of the provisions of the law and confirm to yourself that you are not caught on the wrong side.

. . .

To summarise

- During the last decade, we saw an explosive growth of technology.
- The most notable of all developments is the growth of Artificial Intelligence
- Artificial Intelligence (Machine learning and Deep learning), when paired with other technologies like analytics can transform over 90 percent of what we do and how we do it
- Many jobs are getting obsolete and many other are in the pipeline
- This is leading to another pandemic called skill-gap
- World is getting ready with a strong infrastructure comprising of
- AI powered platforms
- Augmented Reality supported applications
- 3D printing
- Excellent network bandwidth supported by 5G and Wi-Fi 6
- Natural Language Processing enabled applications
- Low-code and no-code development platforms are accelerating implementation of strong computing platforms with an excellent user experience
- Technologies like Natural Language Processing are simplifying the usage of digital technologies
- Technologies like IOT are further enabling an end-to-end automation
- Digital Quotient enables us to see many things differently and provides us with a competitive advantage
- We need to understand three dimensions of Digital Quotient: Personal, Professional, and Family
- Technology can be used very effectively to improve productivity. There are over 100 ready use platforms that can simplify many daily activities we do.

- This has passed the real computing power to the end user
- Information and cyber security incidents are on the rise and calls for awareness of safe computing and responsible usage of technology
- Compliance to privacy laws become more and more stringent and can potentially uproot an offending organization

6

NUMBER QUOTIENT

"It's not what you look at that matters, it's what you see."
- Henry David Thoreau

LEARNING OBJECTIVES

AT THE END of this session, you will be able to

- Understand the need for daily analytics
- Understand the velocity and enormity of data growth
- Appreciate the need to utilise data to your advantage
- Understand the need to develop perceptual acuity
- Learn how to develop perceptual acuity
- Understand the role and application of analytics in government and corporate houses
- Appreciate the developments in AI, ML and DL
- Explore various tools and, KPIs and for data-driven decision making

Our context of intelligence

Here, we are not talking about the general intelligence quotient pertaining to general reasoning, arithmetic and numerical aptitude. That kind of IQ is still essential. However, we need a more critical variant of IQ to excel in this information world.

The modern-day IQ refers more to the following:

- Business Intelligence
- Service Intelligence
- Competitive Intelligence

Leveraging

- Natural human intelligence

Using

- Simple tools

We certainly need the help of trained data scientists and analytics experts to run complex analytics involving massive data. They can produce several insights covering:

- What happened in the past
- What is likely to occur in the future
- What we need to do now

These experts will apply AI and sophisticated algorithms to fetch answers. However, we are referring to an essential self-service; common sense driven insights, to boost our daily productivity. In this chapter, we will explore various methods to achieve this.

How much data is available on the planet?

Human and machine-generated data are growing 10 times faster than traditional business data. Machine-driven data is increasing 50 times more rapidly. Putting it into perspective:

1 Tera Byte = **1,000 gigabytes**

One Zetta Byte: 1 billion TB or 1 trillion GB

One Zetta Byte: 1 followed by 21 zeroes

Total estimated data bytes: 175,000,000,000,000,000,000,000 (21 Zeroes)

In comparison, how many liters of water is there on the planet?

1,260,000,000,000,000,000,000

1 Zetta byte: **21 zero** (Bytes)

1 Sextillion: **21 zeroes**

Total water (in litres)

1.3 Sextillion

Total estimated data I bytes

175 Zetta Bytes

. . .

What are we doing with this data?

When we have a 20/20 vision, we call it regular eyesight. We know about visual acuity and how to measure it. We have contact lenses, spectacles and laser surgeries to improve visual acuity.

- What about our perceptual acuity? Is there a way to measure it?
- If it can be measured what can a person with a 20/20 perceptual acuity see?
- Can a person with a 20/20 perceptual acuity look at a simple excel worksheet and comprehend the information?
- What about our estimation skills?

A simple check of your perception and estimation sense:

- What's the average time spent by three of your direct reports to commute to the office?
- Approximately how many steps do you take from your home to reach an ATM, medical shop, or grocery store?
- Approximately how many complaints and revision requests would you have received in the last month?
- Which were your best and worst productivity weeks last year?
- What went wrong when the productivity hit the floor?

These questions look simple, but many people find it challenging to give reasonably accurate answers.

. . .

Q: Do we have the ability to perceive an impending danger and take proactive steps?

A: What went wrong with epidemic? Why were so many people infected?

What is your perceptual acuity? Good, Bad , or Ugly?

Your ability to find the doors when everyone sees only walls is your perceptual acuity. So, what are we doing with the data available to us? Not much.

> "Errors, like straws, upon the surface flow; He who would search for pearls must dive below."
>
> —John Dryden

Benefits of improved perceptual acuity

Improved perceptual acuity results in the following:

- Increase in revenues
- Improves customer delight
- Reduces costs
- Reduces risks
- Improves customer engagement
- Improves employee engagement

- Shifts us from Reactive to Proactive
- Shifts us from Post-Mortem to Pre-Mortem

What is lowering the perceptual acuity?

The reasons could be the following:

- Imbalanced intellectual humility
- Lack of awareness
- Eleven evils
- Bad consumption habits
- Other deficiencies or lack of willpower

Imbalanced Intellectual Humility

In Chapter 1, we explored the need to balance our intellectual humility. Even a slight imbalance pushes us to either servility or arrogance.

Sometimes it is ok to be servile. Others will identify and correct their behaviour. However, if the attitude tilts towards the arrogance, no one will even come forward to rectify the flaw. This is what is happening in most cases. Several executives believe that they have the right answers.

Lack of awareness

. . .

Lack of awareness about available data and the potential of the data

Lack of awareness about the right tools that can unveil the power of information

We have umpteen success stories that underpin the importance of analytics and the advantages. Technology has been dramatically democratised now. We don't need to pursue complex courses on data science or statistics and master cryptic tools to carry out basic analyses. We have plenty of simple and handy tools to aid us in our everyday life. We will discuss some of these shortly. Fortunately, MS Excel now fits in data curves and has emerged as a robust and mature toolkit for powerful analytics.

But why MS Excel? Old is gold. It does not require introduction or training. The data tab on the ribbon notifies you whenever a new feature is introduced. This may appear like a regular feature unless you look closely. It offers mind-blowing flexibility and simplicity in accomplishing very sophisticated data mining tasks.

Bad consumption habits

Data is always raw. Data needs to be sanitised, validated, and brought in to a functional shape before it can be processed.

Information is what you get when the data is in a semi-processed state. It is still raw. When the source is not validated, it could be toxic too. Consumption of raw foods results in indigestion and constipation. You need to convert the information into insights.

Many times, lack of awareness or reluctance to walk the extra mile pushes people to settle for what is available.

Eleven Evils

We have seen the perils of succumbing to the eleven evils. Tolerating the evils blurs our vision and may result in permanent blindness.

Ability and Willingness

We will address the ability issues shortly. I will demonstrate how simple it is to get the information we need.

We will not discuss the cure for lack of will power.

What are we doing with the current data?

. . .

Ninety percent of the data available on the planet is dark data. Only the rest is available in a useable format. What is dark data? It includes data that is:

- Unstructured
- Physical or semi -electronic
- Not validated

Unstructured data: The data gathered from messages, social media and similar spaces is not structured. Most of the database management systems we use can only work with structured data in fixed formats. Database programmers use Structured Query Language to extract the data. But the world has changed. With some effort, we could transform the data to a consumable state.

Physical: A large chunk of data still exists on paper or as scanned documents. While OCR tools can extract some of it, most of the handwritten papers are lying unexplored. This is because the requirements of Intelligent Character Recognition (ICR) are stringent. However, this is slowly changing due to the right intervention of AI.

Not Validated: If we capture data without proper input validation, most of it will be erroneous. Errors could include spelling mistakes, blanks, duplication or a combination of them.

ANALYTICS IN CITIZEN SERVICES

The government can use the following analytics to improve citizen experience and create various policies.

- Pilferage tracking
- Behavior patterns
- Welfare measures
- Crime prevention
- Improving citizen experience
- Measuring policy effectiveness
- Logistic management of essential services
- Trends in education
- Demand and supply dynamics
- Environmental protection
- Improving healthcare
- Improving medical services
- Pandemic prediction and preparation
- Driving awareness

Many political parties in the world use analytics very effectively to understand the vote bank and formulate winning strategies. They develop selective amnesia the moment they come to power. Some advanced cities in the world use analytics effectively to improve the citizen experience.

Melbourne city shares data on transportations, sensor, property and the like with its citizens. You can find a few on https://data.melbourne.vic.gov.au

Brazil has an app called 'Crime Radar' to create awareness and track crime.

Some cities allow people to track the usage of public lights and other civic services. They even open servicing spots to fix the issues

Some cities have successfully implemented automated fare collection systems through face recognition systems. Many cities in world are being transformed into smart cities, and efforts are underway to collate the data of the residents. Several automation initiatives are being adopted in the country with each of them at different phases of implementation.

Analytics in corporate governance

People analytics for HR

- Workforce planning
- Shift planning
- Talent acquisition
- Employee engagement
- Churn prediction
- Understanding employee behavior
- Inputs for performance evaluations
- Inputs for training needs
- Input for KPI crafting
- NPS

Finalytics for Finance

- Revenue and expense analytics
- Understand billing trends
- To segment customers based on receivables
- To segment vendors based on payables
- Inputs for budgets, capital allocation, and forecasting
- Experience Analytics for Customer Service and Support functions
- SLA trends
- To measure and improve customer experience
- To segment customers
- To understand service trends, bottlenecks, and exceptions

Prospect and customer analytics for Marketing teams

- Understand the lead Propensity
- NPS
- Consumer behavior
- Churn
- Life cycle management

Spend Analytics for Procurement

- Vendor analysis
- Pilferage tracking
- Understand billing trends
- To segment vendors based on payables

Fraud Analytics Risk management and Compliance

- Fraud profiling
- Fraud prevention
- Inputs for devising controls
- Direction for enhancing the surveillance
- Outlier, anomalies and exception tracking

Product Analytics for Product Management , IT development and UI/UX teams

- Measuring and reporting product usage trends.
- A design feature that matters to users.

Learning Analytics for Training department

- Skill Gap analysis
- Training Need Identification

Performance Analytics for Top management using several dashboards

InfoSec Analytics for the Whole IT team to observe the trends and vulnerabilities in the application, network, APIS, and computing environment

Large organisations may have invested in specialised tools or hired relevant people. However, globally only 15 percent of the organisations have employed such mature technology. A whopping 85 percent of organisations and executives are still deprived. Fortunately, over 80 percent of the reports and dashboards mentioned above can be generated in-house using simple tools. It does not require any coding or data science skills.

Steps to start self-help intelligence dashboards

Steps:

- Identify KPIs for talent acquisition
- Select the right tools
- Identify data streams and validate the data
- Analyse, automate and test

Performance metrics

While there are several tools available to do the number-crunching, we must have reliable and practical KPIs. If we know what we need to do, we can always figure out how to do it.

What is a KPI? Key Performance Indicator is a measure that tells you how effectively you can accomplish a goal. Let's assume you want to travel from Mumbai to Pune on an urgent business trip. You don't want to drive because you are not familiar with the route and traffic conditions. Therefore, you decide to hire a driver and interview ten drivers. But how do you know which driver is good? It would be useful if you have the following information about the drivers:

- Number of trips they have made on the highway (Experience)
- Number of trips between Mumbai and Pune (Awareness of the route)
- Average mileage (Economy)
- Number of accidents he has been in (Safety)
- Knowledge of routes
- The average number of breaks taken per 100 km (Does he need a break for every 10 km?)
- Total traffic penalties paid

This is a KPI for selection.

Once you have made the selection, you can just measure one KPI - average speed. It will tell you whether you can reach the destination on time.

Instead, what if you keep measuring the following every hour?

- Pressure in all the tyres
- Total fuel in the tank

You can measure them every ten minutes. But will it take you any closer to the destination?

Setting the right performance metric is as important as the goal itself. Many people end up measuring the wrong metric and get confused between activity and result.

The following are the indicative KPIs to measure the effectiveness of HR function

- Revenue per employee
- Employee churn rate
- Cost of attrition
- HR to employee ratio
- The average cost per hire
- Desire to hire time

Similarly, the following are the sample KPIs for business effectiveness:

- Space utilisation
- SLA compliance in percentage
- Revisions done in percentage
- Number of open complaints
- Billing fulfilment
- Revenue per employee
- Win ratio
- Upselling rates
- Client concentration
- NPS score – Client

- NPS score – Employee
- The total cost of IT

Several online KPI libraries can generate very functional metrics. Sounds good? But what are life KPIs? Let's begin by understanding the following:

- Percentage of allotted investment
- Percentage of un-allotted investment
- Percentage of deviation

You can investment three of your scarce resources:

- Your time
- Energy
- Money

You need to invest all three of them wisely. You need to plan, allocate, monitor and fine-tune continuously. A wise time and energy investment will give you immense satisfaction. In most cases, this investment ensures that you get the third factor also, in abundance.

Every morning, when you wake up, decide one thing: How you propose to invest the time available to you today. Are you spending or investing? Spending is a loose affair that does not fetch you any returns on the investment. It is a wasted effort. If you think there is an RoI, how much is it and for how long? What is the allocation?

. . .

At the end of the day before you sleep recap the three KPIs: Percentage of allotted investment, percentage of un-allotted investment and the percentage of deviation. Do this every day and realise the potential to bring about transformations. This is the first step to sustained growth.

Find the right tools

There are over a dozen free and paid KPI metric tools in the market. Each of them come loaded with KPIs for popular industries, dashboard samples, integrations and everything else required for developing a powerful dashboard.

Take a look at the following:

Free: Open-source / Community editions

https://count.ly
http://metabase.com/

Paid:

https://www.geckoboard.com
https://www.klipfolio.com
https://www.cluvio.com

Identify data streams and validate the data

Depending on the type of analytics you want to do, data streams can stem from multiple sources. For instance, if you want to build a sales and marketing dashboard Google Analytics could be accessed from a corresponding Gmail account.

Similarly, if you want to build a product development dashboard, data can come from issue tracking tools such as Jira and development tools like visual studio. You can add the primary HR database to link the respective resources. Each of these tools above can integrate into multiple sources and also validate the data. The idea is to start small and advance.

Analyse, automate and test

Each of these tools give us the readymade templates and dashboards for analysis based on the key metrics you finalise. You can use tools such as Zapier and IFTTT to link these applications and automate the data flow.

Once you build these reports, do parallel testing for at least a week before you bring it to force. Having said that, we could try to achieve the necessary results using just our good old MS Excel.

One of the most useful and powerful books you could read in your life would be 'Four disciplines of execution' through which management guru, Steven R Covey, gave the following disciplines to the world:

- Discipline 1: Focus on the wildly important.
  Exceptional execution starts with narrowing the focus.
- Discipline 2: Act on the lead measures.
- Discipline 3: Keep a compelling scoreboard.

- Discipline 4: Create a cadence of accountability.

This book had a profound impact on my life. My real career growth started when I understood that execution is the only thing that matters. This chapter tries to teach you Discipline 3: Keeping a scoreboard.

Analytics sampler

In this section, we will take up recruitment as a case study and will see how Excel-based analytics will help us in the process of acquiring the right talent. We want to measure the following:

- Which recruiter is efficient?
- Which project manager has the most requirement or attrition rate?
- What is the requirement for each position and the number of recruiters available?
- Which is the most efficient channel to source?

We will measure the following KPIs:

- Attrition Rate: Recruiter
- Attrition Rate: Project Manager
- Attrition Rate: Function
- Attrition Rate: Level
- Desire to hire: Recruiter
- Desire to hire: Position
- Desire to hire: Channel
- The average cost per hire

- The average cost per hire per channel

In addition to the above KPIs, we will also have two more dashboards

- Who is hiring whom
- Recruitment Funnel

Who is hiring whom: gives us the efficiency of each recruiting manager. Whether we use analytics and motivate employees or not, there will still be some smart candidates who are always talented, fully engaged, self-motivated and therefore very efficient.

The smartness of the leader lies in

- Spotting the spark
- Recognising and rewarding the talent
- Taking their help to boost the overall productivity

In the previous chapters, we saw four categories of people. Those in Category A will know all shortcuts and smart ways of working. You need to pair those falling under Category A with B. Your job is also to ensure that Category D is identified and dispensed with quickly.

The Recruitment Funnel gives us an inherent sense of what is happening at each milestone.

- Total resumes
- Candidates filtered
- Interviews conducted
- Selected
- Offers released
- Joined

It will be quicker to identify gaps and bottleneck areas. You can download the template from your online work-area: https://gem.prowessca.com. You can use your data and get all dashboards free. You can also watch an online video on how to do it from scratch.

Most people have a general belief that HR is responsible for all the above functions. Therefore, why should leaders like us bother about them?

Well, managing the support function well is one of the critical KPIs of a leader. The more you know about your service provider, the better you can support them and the quicker the results.

TO SUMMARISE

- Develop curiosity
- Never let the eleven evils or humility imbalance cloud your perspective
- Change your data consumption habits
- Convert data to information and information to insight
- Never consume raw data
- Validate your assumptions
- Create KPIs and metrics
- Start estimating and predicting

- Create a mental benchmark
- Always attempt to listen to the data hums. They are the most melodious
- Data can separate logic and emotions
- When you can differentiate with data, world distinguishes you from the ordinary
- Data-driven leadership is the most practical and sustainable method
- Start estimating and validating
- Start with the primary KPIs and metrics
- Technology has been democratised. Leverage it
- Collaborate with a technical expert if needed
- Challenge yourself to discover one new trend or insight every month

7

SUMMIT

Om Sarveshaam Svastir-Bhavatu |
Sarveshaam Shaantir-Bhavatu |
Sarveshaam Purnnam-Bhavatu |
Sarveshaam Manggalam-Bhavatu |
Om Shaantih Shaantih Shaantih ||

May there be Well-Being in All,
May there be Peace in All,
May there be Fulfilment in All,
May there be Auspiciousness in All,
Om Peace! Peace! Peace!

REWIND

REMEMBER various types of people we discussed in the first chapter?

- Some people make things happen
- Some watch

- Some wonder what has happened.

I hope you are now aware of who these people are and what strengths and shortcomings each of them has. Did you also realise that there is a fourth category as well? These are people who stop things from happening. These toxic people at work comprise of consultants, self-proclaimed experts, free advisors and unsolicited critics. Be aware and keep away from them.

We have learned the following:

- There are four quotients to master to achieve ultimate success
- We have seen five psychometrics that profiles our personality and reveal our strengths
- We have also seen the inner evils that cause severe damage
- We have learned how to install the Mind Positioning System, set our goals, and position our locus
- We have understood what our roots are and how to strengthen them
- We have learned various internal and interpersonal skills to position our competencies
- You should now be able to:
- Use your GRIT to achieve your goals
- Open up your communication strategies
- Make your presentations SIMPLE
- Follow the proven PATH for customer delight
- HEAL your team members and wounded clients proactively
- Follow the most SUIT-able method to resolve team conflicts

- CALM down your fears

FINDING THE PURPOSE

We discussed the goal-setting in Chapter 2. We also learned how to use the GRIT method to get there.

But goals are always for the short term. They help you attain temporary pleasures, give you a sense of achievement and alignment. Goals could include getting a promotion, upgrading your car, phone, or home or picking up a new skill. Once you complete these, your heart sets a bigger target and forces you to go after it. Goals add spice to life.

However, we need to find a purpose and keep pushing the envelope. They could be professional, personal or spiritual. When you set an appropriate target and achieve it, your reputation outlives your life. The Japanese have identified a simple method to stay happy. They call it 'Ikigai.' Ikigai refers to a reason for living and staying happy.

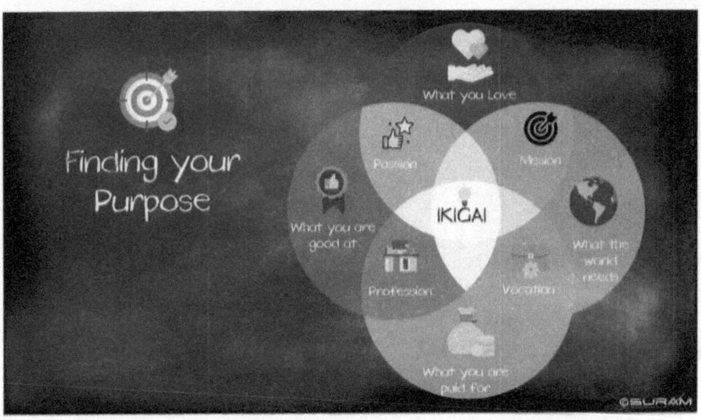

We often experience the following states during the career progression:

- What you are good at
- What you love
- What does the world need
- What you are getting paid for

It is also essential that we have the following:

- Delight
- Satisfaction
- Excitement
- Money

Note that money does not activate your excitement or delight you for long. If that were the case, all the rich people should be happy and content while the poor gloomy and miserable. But we often observe reverse trends. It is not practical to get them all on to a single plate.

- What you love + What the world wants = Mission
- What the world wants + What you are paid for = Vocation
- What you are paid for + What you are good at = Profession
- What you are good at + What you love = Passion

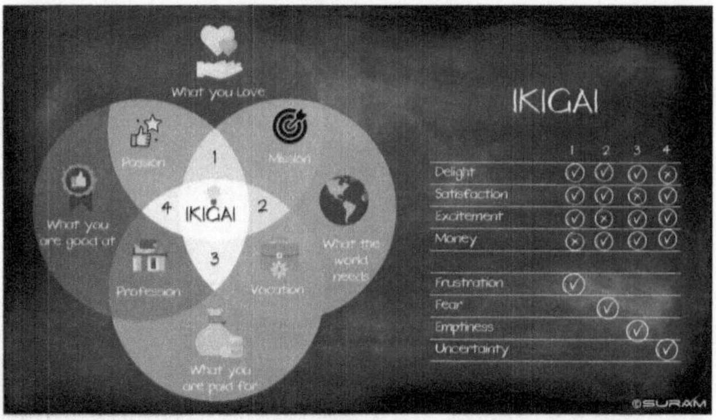

The intersection of passion and mission gives you delight because you are driving your mission and pursuing your passions. But since you have not found anyone to pay you for it, you get frustrated after a while.

The intersection of mission and vocation will bode well for some time. You get a good feeling because you are doing what you love and the world needs. You are also getting paid for it. Seems good. You attain some satisfaction. However, since you are not good at what you currently do, you are always outdone by a better performer.

So, you decide to take up the next option and try to do what you are good at instead of what you love doing. This will also be exciting for some time but you will be engulfed by emptiness because there is nothing in it that you like.

Then you move to the next block to try to do something that you are good at and also like. You also find someone who will pay you for it. You are getting money for sure, but since this is not what the world needs, you start feeling the uncertainty. You may become irrelevant at any point.

So the best option is to move to the centre which can give you all four of them.

Engage your GENIE

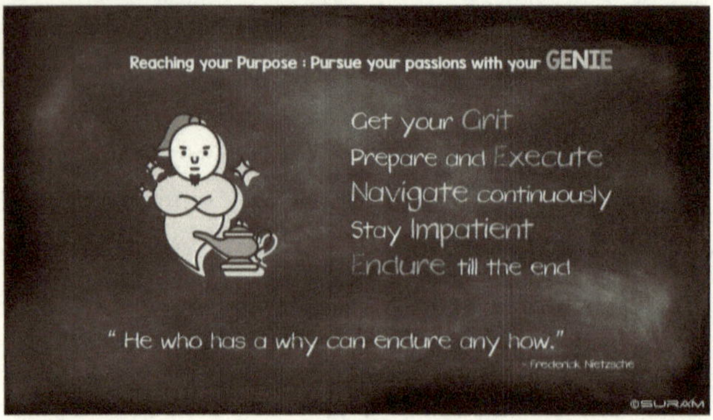

How do you pursue the purpose? Well. You understood the method to pursue your goals. The process is almost similar but with some additional steps. Here is a five step formula to achieve your life's mission.

- Get your **GRIT**
- Prepare and **execute**
- **Navigate** continuously
- Stay **impatient**
- **Endure** till the end

This method is equally applicable for any large project.

Stimulate your creative brain with this process

. . .

Short of ideas? Not able to think of innovative methods to solve a problem or find a solution? Reboot your creative brain with the following process

Necessity is the mother of invention. You need to either crave to achieve something or create a compulsion to trigger your thought process. Our brains are not normally receptive to anything other than cricket and politics. If nothing else excites us, we settle down in front of the idiot box. But how did we move to higher levels of digitisation and automation in India? How did we adopt technology so fast? The technology adoption at least for Fintech happened during the following phases:

- Demonetisation
- Lockdown

You must have realised that many people switched to UPI or PayTM after demonetisation. But who were the first to adopt to this change? Wallet transactions were mainly embraced by street hawkers and other roadside vendors. But why? It was a question of survival for them. With no currency available for transaction, they had no other means but to accept a digital transaction. Could they read? Were they proficient in handling smartphones prior to this? Do they vile away their time on social media? The answer to all this is a big no. But still, they were the first to adopt and push the usage.

Similarly, we have started taking many technology related initiatives during the lockdown period. These are primarily because we were deprived of the basics. In the case of a street vendor, he will have to go to bed hungry in case he does not do minimum business. There are many leadership case studies on under privileged people and their lifestyles.

Enough of introduction to the main topic. You need to practice frugality to trigger the creative juices in your brain. I invented a 'two wallet' method for the same.

I have two wallets in my pocket. One a physical one and the other virtual. The real wallet contains part of my monthly income for family expenses. The money in my virtual wallet is what I earn everyday as a token for good behaviour or conduct. In reality, this is what you truly earn.

Now, whenever you need to bring about a change or attempt anything new, rollback the token funds. You will soon become bankrupt and will need to put your personal gratification on hold until you earn some more. This could include staying off coffee, smoke or booze that you normally enjoy. This puts severe pressure on your brain to devise a way to earn.

You can always achieve productivity through frugality. You can learn the most important life lessons through induced bankruptcy. Sounds crazy but it works. You could give it a try. It will be effective as long as you are serious and sincere. You cannot borrow or get someone else to sponsor. Try this and let me know.

Meet yourself and understand yourself

- What are your goals and ambitions?

- Remember, your aims or priorities could be short-term, mid-term or long term.
- Your priorities and preferences change from time to time.
- Understand your priorities and preferences.
- What you aim for and crave today might seem like a trap after a year or a decade.
- Therefore, you need to build meaningful dreams.
- You will always be working on fulfilling dreams. The question is, whose dreams are you working for?
- Know yourself first, wholly.
- Surf your inner self fifty times more than you surf the internet (social media, chats, messaging, and various other distractions).
- Complete the psychometric evaluations and understand your strengths and talents.
- What do you want to achieve? Start with an end in mind.
- What do you want to change? Start with self – conquer inner enemies.
- Joy is in leading a regret-free and guilt-free life.
- Focus on terminal hours.

Define success

- What is your definition of success and failure?
- Success is more about how you perceive failure and how you cope with failures and setbacks. Perseverance plays a pivotal role.
- Do not compare yourself with others while setting your life goals. You may draw inspiration but understand that success is personalised and unique.
- Success always comes with caveats and after sacrifices.

- Success demands barter. What are you ready to forego?
- What is the price you are willing to pay to pursue the goals?
- Ultimately, you need to balance your professional and personal life.
- Those who don't understand this will eventually suffer success instead of celebrating it.
- Be failure-friendly. Once you overcome the fear of failure, you will get very close to success.
- Success should result in realising your real well-being targets also.
- Remember your real assets are always intangible. Knowledge, health and relationships are your real wealth and possessions to take pride in.
- The rest of the possessions are temporary and worthless. These three possessions set you free while other tangible or material possessions lock you up.
- Your gain cannot be at the cost of someone else's loss or misery.
- Real success is in leading a regret-free and guilt-free life after you have accomplished your goals.
- Know what you want to achieve.
- Know what you want to concentrate on improving
- The goal of goal-setting: Long-term vision gives you the direction, drive, emotional balance and focus.
- Look at the most crooked politicians. Most of them may not be well educated and knowledgeable, but all of them know one thing clearly: their time is finite and the wealth goals are infinite.
- The rule for the rest of the rules: Customer>Organisation>Team>Individual.
- Develop hunger sensors and taste buds for your brain.
- Authentic leadership is all about getting people to follow you willingly.
- Declare 10 percent of your time as terminal hours and focus on achieving.

- Giving precedes getting.
- Unlike the stomach, the brain does not trigger hunger pangs. It starves silently and dies eventually. Feed your brain. It deserves to get some attention and partiality.
- In the inbox of God, you are a message or actionable item. There are many spammers around and the inbox is full of futile conversations. You get wrongly tagged and grouped.
- Set up a robust reporting system.
- Set your productivity standards.
- Decide what to do before breakfast.
- Focus on emerging technology trends.
- Gift yourself something every day.
- Meet the most crucial people every day.
- People who look for control end up in a situation where their bodies don't obey.
- Read on Kindle and listen to Audible.

Your competition, enemies, friends and guards

- Always compete with yourself.
- Always ask and take help.
- Don’t make decisions based on assumptions.
- Stay completely focused and pay attention to detail.
- Aim for 10 percent improvement each month.
- Invest at least 10 percent of your time and income on yourself.
- Resistance is your only arch-rival. Fight and win the war every day. You always lose when your resistance wins.
- Prefer education rather than entertainment.
- Unlike the stomach, the brain does not trigger hunger pangs. It starves silently and dies eventually.
- Your credibility is your best pal. Protect your credibility as eye-lids protect your eyes.

- Focus on your achievement meter than the applause meter.
- Understand that we are mortals. Declare 10 percent of your time as terminal hours and focus on achieving.
- The more you connect with the needs of others, the more the success will get linked to you.
- Try to adjust your biological clock. Morning is the best time to pursue your passions.

Your possessions

- Take care of your finances. Start investing early and regularly.
- Subscribe to a Systematic Invest Plan and forget this investment.
- Start with a simple balance sheet: What did you earn and lose today. What are you grateful for today?
- Invest at least 10 percent of your time and income on yourself.
- Protect your credibility as the eye-lids protect your eyes.
- Remember, your real assets are always intangible. Knowledge, health, and relationships are your real wealth and possessions to take pride in. The rest of the possessions are too temporary and much worthless.
- Tangible or material possessions lock you up.
- Differentiate between skill and sense.
- Don't let your skills bite you.
- Understand that we are mortals.
- Find your *IKIGAI*.
- Aim for10 percent improvement every month.

JAIN FORGIVENESS DAY

Jains have a forgiveness day. Just the way business people have accounts closing day, they have a score settling day. They forget all problems created by others and forgive them. Similarly, they request others to forgive them for known and unknown sins and shortcomings. They call it *Micchami Dukkadam*

It means:

I forgive all living beings. May all souls forgive me. I am in friendly terms with all, and I have no animosity towards any soul. May all my faults be dissolved. This is such a noble practice. We must practice this every weekend. This is not to suggest that you beat your colleague up on Saturday and tell him *Micchami Dukkadam* on Sunday!

Forgiveness is the greatest virtue that you can inculcate. This brings us to the end of this course. I wish you all the best and grand success!

Om Sarveshaam Svastir-Bhavatu |
Sarveshaam Shaantir-Bhavatu |
Sarveshaam Purnnam-Bhavatu |
Sarveshaam Manggalam-Bhavatu |
Om Shaantih Shaantih Shaantih ||

May there be well-being in all,
May there be peace in all,
May there be fulfilment in all,
May there be auspiciousness in all,
Om peace! Peace! Peace!

8

ABOUT THE AUTHOR

SuRaM, **Su**bba **Ra**o **M**ukkavilli is an author and serial entrepreneur.

He is the founder of the following organisations:

- www.ProwessCA.com, an e-Learning organisation.
- www.Skillculture.in A social platform for skill development.

During the last 30 years of his career, Suram has set up various business lines, worked with corporate giants and governments, and set up several complex enterprise IT platforms.

He is an expert in people and process alignment, business transformation, and strategic IT management.

Before writing this book, Suram has authored two books on presentation and communication skills. His first book, "SlideSpin" has received the Global eBook Award, California, USA in Silver Category in 2015.

Before setting up Prowessca, he worked as a CTO at KFin Technologies and as an Executive Director at Karvy Insurance Repository.

He can be reached at sr@suram.me.

THANK YOU

Thank you for reading my book.

You can access bonus material, templates and toolkits on https://gem.prowessca.com

If you liked this book, please leave a positive review on Amazon and share this book with your friends on social platforms.

I wish you good luck!

www.ingramcontent.com/pod-product-compliance
Lightning Source LLC
Chambersburg PA
CBHW050012170726
48282CB00025B/379
9789354079351